7-12.16 ∅

CREATING YOUR RESUME

A Step-by-Step Guide to Write Your First Competitive Resume

by **Kathryn Troutman** *with* **Paulina Chen** *Editor & Designer*

Federal Career Training Institute

1012 Edmondson Avenue, Catonsville, MD 21228
Phone: (888) 480-8265
www.fedjobtraining.com
Email: firstresume@fedjobtraining.com

Printed in the United States of America
ISBN-13: 978-0-9861421-0-9
ISBN-10: 986142107
Copyright © 2016 by Kathryn Troutman

Publication Team:

Developmental editor, book design, and cover design: Paulina Chen, Ashburn, VA
Resume sample editor and lesson consultant: Rachel Blazucki, Teacher, Baltimore, MD
Resume designs and templates: Paulina Chen, Hloom.com, Molly Nix, and Microsoft Word
Photographs: Cecile Walton, college student, Ellicott City, MD
Student book consultant: Addison J. Chen, high school student, Ashburn, VA
Proofreader: Pam Sikora
Indexer: Pilar Wyman

From Kathryn Troutman, Author and Publisher:

A future career plan ideally starts in high school. Early passions, skills, interests, jobs, internships, and courses can result in a total career plan. I want to thank my kids, Emily, Lori, and Chris, and all of their friends for inspiring me every day to encourage students and young people to WRITE THEIR FIRST RESUME for their career and for the rest of their life! Also, I want to thank AJ Chen for contributing to the book design and the LEVELS of resume writing and job search success; Paulina Chen for her beautiful designs of words, graphics, and resumes; Rachel Blazucki, an 8th grade teacher and former federal employee and writer, for her inspiration to keep this project alive for high school English classes; and the military employment readiness and transition counselors who are encouraging transitioning military, spouses and family members to write a correct and current-style, up-to-date resume to manage and improve their careers—during their military life and after. Thank you to Hloom.com, a free online resume template resource, for granting us permission to use several of their wonderful template designs in this book.

INTRODUCTION

Need to write your first resume? Not sure how?

Let us take you through the different levels of pulling together your very first resume and all the way through to preparing for your interview. Our goal in this book is to make this adventure as simple as possible for you. Many times we will just show you how to do it with examples rather than tell you how., but we'll also tell you enough to point you in the right direction.

Even if you just make it through Level 1, you WILL have a basic resume that you can use! Each level beyond that will continue to improve upon what you have and give you a better chance of getting hired.

LEVEL ONE:

Draft Your Basic Resume

LEVEL TWO:

The Big Three

LEVEL THREE:

Pick Your Format

LEVEL FOUR::

Make Your Resume
Straight Fire

LEVEL FIVE:

Write a Legit
Cover Letter

LEVEL SIX:

Apply for Jobs
Like a Pro

LEVEL SEVEN:

Interview on Point

LEVEL EIGHT:

Follow Up:
Keep It 100

TABLE OF CONTENTS

SAMPLE RESUMES IN THIS BOOK

Photo by Cecile Walton

draft your basic resume

Photo by Cecile Walton

WHAT IS A RESUME?

A resume is a summary of your high school, college, and other training, activities, volunteer and paid experience, and skills. Whether you are writing a resume for a job or internship, applying for college, or completing a class assignment, this resume will be the first of many resumes that you will write in your life.

THE BASIC RESUME

The first step in writing your resume is simply to start writing! Just get your basic information down on paper. We'll call this your "basic resume," and we will continue to improve on this draft in the next levels.

TAKE ACTION!

Start writing using the outline on the next page and the samples in this book.

basic resume sections

Personal Information – Your name, address, email address, and telephone number. Make your name the biggest font, so it is what stands out the most. Think about how the information will influence an employer's view of you, and make sure your email address and cell message are appropriate! Your future employer doesn't want to hire partygirl01@gmail.com, so make a new one if you need to.

Objective/Academic Goal – If you are applying for a job, internship, co-op, or special program, you should include an objective section in your resume. Focus your objective on the job or internship for which you are applying.

If you are applying to college, you can do an Academic Goal section, which can include the major and any special programs you'd like to pursue.

Skills – This section gives you a chance to list your special skills. Whether you know html coding, app development, Adobe Photoshop, music editing, or computerized sewing, list it in the special skills section.

Education – This section will include the name, city, and state of your high school or college, as well as your expected graduation date. Add your GPA if it is over 2.5. List your specialized courses in a separate paragraph, so that the employer or college recruiter can see your unique courses and interests. Add your language skills, courses, and levels of ability.

Honors and Awards – Your honors and awards show that you have skills and are dedicated. List your honors and awards and include the date. This section could include awards such as National Honor Society, Perfect Attendance, etc.

Extracurricular Activities – By looking at this section, employers and admissions staff can learn about your involvement in your school and outside activities. Include sports teams and clubs. Be sure to name any leadership positions that you have held on sports teams or in clubs.

Work Experience - The paid and unpaid jobs you have had while in school will be important for future employers, human resources staff, and college recruiters. They will look at the length of time you worked, including the number of hours per week. It is important to describe your duties and any accomplishments you may have achieved.

Volunteer and Community Service – Be sure to include all of your volunteer and community service jobs on your resume. Include the duties that you held for each position.

Language, Travel, and Personal Interests – This information contains extra details that just give a little more information about you. If you can speak another language, that could be impressive for an employer or college (but don't exaggerate if you can't!). Travel experiences can demonstrate global knowledge and experiences. Your personal interests are added details that can say more about you and can create great conversation in an interview.

KMJ

KYLIE
MARIE
JENNINGS

124 Hana Avenue
Haiku, HI 99999
(555) 555-9999
E-mail: bigwave@net.net

EDUCATION

HALL COLLEGE PREPARATORY, Olinda, Maui, Hawaii

Expect to graduate in 20xx

Headmaster's List, GPA: 3.9 (20xx–20xx school year)

Academic Courses: Japanese I, Spanish IV, Honors Physics, Pre-Calculus

Activities: Member, Cross-Country and Track Team, Second in Maui County, 20xx

WORKSHOPS

Smyth School of Art, Washington, DC, summer 20xx–Studio Art and Photography

Costa Rica, Central America, summer 20xx–Spanish-Language Immersion

EMPLOYMENT

MAUI RETAIL CORP., Lahaina, Maui, 20xx–present

Retail Sales/Computer Assistant to the Regional Manager

- Perform computer research concerning inventory, costs, and store information.
- Research competitive companies, products, and catalogs via the Internet.
- Manipulate online data to create sales and financial reports.
- Develop formulas and create Excel spreadsheets, graphs, and reports for management and financial analysis by managers.
- Conduct retail sales, friendly customer service, inventory control, and merchandising.
- Communicate with retail store managers about inventory orders and shipments.
- Research and problem-solve missing products

SKILLS

Languages: Fluent Spanish; currently studying Japanese

Computers: Microsoft Suite, Online Point of Sale Computer Systems, Lightroom

INTERESTS

Extensive travel in the United States and Central America

Hawaiian culture and history

Philosophy and environmental sciences

Outdoor activities, including hiking, camping, and biking

PERSONAL QUALITIES

Dependable, hardworking, motivated, sincere, and analytical

Challenged by learning and new experiences

2

the big three

READY TO TAKE YOUR RESUME TO THE NEXT LEVEL?

Make your resume super impressive by adding **the big three:**

 skills

 accomplishments

 keywords

skills

Tell others what you can do! Think of skills as being something you do well. In general, skills can be divided into two categories: technical skills and soft skills.

TECHNICAL SKILLS

Having specific technical skills can help you get a corresponding job, so they are often referred to as job-related skills. Being extremely clear about your technical skills is important. A potential employer will appreciate seeing a list of these skills.

EXAMPLES

SKILLS

- Knowledge of construction principles, basic building systems, and project management.
- Computer Skills: Proficient in Word, Excel, and PowerPoint; 4-D, AutoDesk Revit, Microsoft Project, and OnScreen Takeoff. Ability to use Excel to assist with takeoffs and cost management.

TECHNICAL SKILLS SUMMARY

Automotive repair/restoration, drive train/heating/AC, and diagnostics and electrical skills.
Skilled analyst and problem-solver.
Rebuild and restore custom automobiles, four-wheelers; award-winner.
Computer skills: Microsoft Office, Excel, and Access

SKILLS SUMMARY
Analytical skills
Schematic readings and manuals
Computer repair, networking, security setup
Strong technical and diagnostic skills
Leadership and communications skills
Keyboarding skills: 40 wpm

SOFT SKILLS

These are skills that are part of your personality, such as being organized or being friendly. You might not realize it, but you have many soft skills. Describing your soft skills is a good way to make yourself more appealing in the job market.

EXAMPLES

Adaptive Skills

Adaptive skills are also called personal skills. These skills are part of your personality. They help you adapt to different situations.

- Enthusiastic
- Energetic
- Friendly
- Outgoing
- Honest
- Dependable
- Physically strong and possessing stamina
- Able to learn quickly
- Sincere
- Patient and calm
- Empathetic (caring)
- Able to get along with coworkers
- Competitive
- Willing to work hard

Transferable Skills

Transferable skills are also called general skills. These are skills that can be used in many jobs.

- Finishing assignments on time
- Working with people
- Flexibility
- Handling many projects at once (multitasking)
- Expressing yourself through art, music, dance, writing
- Staying organized
- Following instructions
- Paying attention to detail
- Speaking before groups
- Leading a club
- Writing clearly
- Member of a team or team leader

TAKE ACTION!

Find 5-7 really important skills that you have to offer and make sure to include them in your resume.

Photo by Cecile Walton

accomplishments

Accomplishments tell people how extraordinary you are and why they should hire you.

For example, a high school student recently completed a half-marathon in all 50 states to raise money for disadvantaged students in his community. Another student became the valedictorian in her high school and received a full scholarship to college—while she was homeless.

Tell an effective story about your accomplishment, and try to hit these points:

- When have I faced a particularly difficult challenge at school or work or while volunteering?

- What did I do to overcome the challenge?

- What positive outcome happened as a result of what I did?

EXAMPLES

Built a 1970 Firebird. Assembled and disassembled the vehicle to the frame.
Aaron Smith – page 19

Won People's Choice Award in local 4 x 4 show for 1978 Chevy Truck
Calvin Kline - page 21

Nominee for "Scholar Athlete" for National Football Foundation
Thomas Garner – page 25

Titlist Junior Tour, PGA Middle Atlantic Section. MIAA Champion.
Matthew Manowitz – page 27

AP classes – a great list!
Molly Jackson – page 29

Finalist – Film Festival; Art Showcase in Row Home Lit; National Art Honor Society; GT/AP courses
Cece Callahan – page 23

Editor-in-Chief, Phoenix Literary Arts Magazine; Debate National Competitor;
Winner of Redmond College's "Women Writing About Women" Competition
Emily K. Thompson – page 31

Received Aloha Award for Customer Services, Hawaii Park Center
Ronald Milestone – page 33

Created new menu to pair food with over five different types of beer. Proposed new supplier to
the owner, who agreed. A local farm provided fresh local produce and resulted in cost savings.
Ryan Abel – page 36

JROTC Member, recognized for leadership and outstanding attendance award
Nathan Brown – page 41

TAKE ACTION!

Think of 2-3 accomplishments.
Summarize them in 1-2 sentences
and add to your resume.

keywords

Keywords are the most important words for a particular company or position. If you add certain keywords to your resume, you will get better results from your resume. The following are samples of keywords taken from internship and job advertisements. You can review these examples to get an idea of how to find keywords on your own.

Keywords for a **Day Care Internship**

Melody Day Care is looking for an individual to be our day care intern at a growing day care center. The individual must possess patience and skill at working with young children and have experience with ensuring safety, discipline, and structure while giving creative learning opportunities. We are seeking someone with a caring and nurturing attitude in classroom and play activities who is able to follow curriculum and work to ensure learning goals are met through activities, small groups, and one-on-one teaching.

KEYWORDS: Patience, skill working with young children, safety, discipline, creative learning, caring, nurturing, follow curriculum to meet learning goals

Keywords for **Zoo Visitor Center Positions**

Friends of the National Zoo, an exciting, dynamic, and diversified nonprofit organization located at the National Zoo, is holding a job fair to meet energetic, friendly, courteous, and outgoing team players for the following positions: Information Aides, Retail Sales Clerks, Food Service Associates, Parking Cashiers, and much more. Punctuality is required.

KEYWORDS: Energetic, friendly, courteous, outgoing team player, information aide, retail sales, punctuality

Keywords for **Kid's Merchandise Sales Positions**

Tree Top Kids, a neighborhood toy store, is looking for energetic sales associates to join its fun-filled staff with a primary focus in the book department. Applicants must enjoy being around children, must be attentive to detail, possess strong organizational skills, and be comfortable using computers. Responsibilities include receiving deliveries and stock in computer, merchandising and shelving products, and communicating with vendors regarding damaged/ missing products. Applicants would also be trained to work on the sales floor, assisting customers and ringing sales through the register. Must be available mornings and afternoons. It's a great position to learn all aspects of the book business from checking in the new inventory to hands-on experience with the customers!

KEYWORDS: Energetic sales associate, enjoy children, attentive to detail, strong organizational skills, computers, merchandising, shelving products, sales, assisting customers, customer services

Keywords for **Airport Team Members**

Virgin America is a new travel brand that challenges industry norms in an attempt to deliver a more human travel experience for the domestic traveler. Guest Services is a team of energetic, focused, and flexible people who have fun at what they do. Our role is to provide our guests with personalized service dedicated to ensuring that the entire travel experience is enjoyable and hassle free. The Airport Guest Services Team Member reports to the Station Supervisor, participates in a "we" environment, and is responsible for customer service at the airport. The Airport Guest Service Team Member must be an assertive self-starter who proactively assumes responsibility for the airline's operational integrity and one who takes action to keep the airline safe, on time, and consistent with our values. The Team Member must be highly organized, focused, and multitask oriented with the ability to prioritize tasks. The position requires quick thinking and in-depth knowledge of overall operations.

KEYWORDS: Energetic, focused, flexible, Guest Services Team Member, customer service, assertive self-starter, proactively assumes responsibility, highly organized, multitasking, ability to prioritize, quick thinking

Keywords for an **Upscale Grocery Store Manager**

Patriot Fred's is looking for part-time crew members in Virginia Beach, VA to work in our grocery store! If you like people, love food, are ambitious and adventuresome, enjoy smiling, and have a strong sense of values, Patriot Fred's is definitely for you. Come be a part of the excitement! Our crew members participate in all aspects of store operations including operating registers, customer service, product receiving, display building, and stocking… but most important, our crew is responsible for making sure that our customers have a truly terrific shopping experience. Who we are looking for: the ideal crew member works with a sense of urgency, loves food, enjoys a physically active work environment, and has a fun, positive personality.

KEYWORDS: Like people, love food, ambitious, adventuresome, enjoy smiling, strong sense of values, crew member, operating register, customer services, product receiving, display building, stocking, physically active, fun positive personality

TAKE ACTION!

Find 5-7 keywords to add to your resume. If you are invited to an interview, review the keywords to make sure you are ready to mention some of these words in the interview as well.

pick your format

ALL RESUMES ARE NOT THE SAME.

There are many opportunities for work, internships, training, and community service during your high school years and beyond; however, not all resumes are created equal. Depending on what you'd like to do with your resume (apply for a job, enlist in the military, etc.), each resume should be individually focused by listing additional specific skills, experience, interests, and courses that would help you stand out.

The resume formats and career ideas covered in this book are the following:

◆ **Technical Training / Certification Resume**

◆ **College Acceptance Resume:** A resume that you can send with your college application and use to apply for scholarships based on performance, grades, and experience. This type of resume could pay off big in the form of scholarship dollars.

◆ **Internship Resume:** A resume that is focused toward the internship program, specialized experience, and mission of the organization you want to intern with. Internships can be either paid or unpaid.

◆ **Job Resume:** A resume that will help you get a job or enter a work-study or co-op program. This resume presents the best employment and job skills you have to offer. Jobs and work-study and co-op positions are usually paid.

◆ **Military Resume:** A resume that features ROTC experience, leadership, discipline, teamwork, sports, grades, and other skills of interest to the U.S. military services. You can also use this type of resume with scholarship requests for help with tuition, books, and other reimbursements.

◆ **Federal Student Jobs Resume:** The federal resume is similar to the resumes in this book, but it can be longer (length can be up to three pages), needs to match qualifications and skills from the USAJOBS government job announcement, and must include all of the information required by USAJOBS.

TECHNICAL TRAINING/CERTIFICATION RESUME

Technical training programs consist both of classwork and paid employment or an internship. These programs teach subjects such as automotive technology, computer graphics and design, accounting, and paralegal work. You might receive a certificate that can help you get a job in a specific technical field.

Military Family Member Pursuing an Automotive Career with a Racing Team: Aaron Smith

Aaron Smith is a "military family member" who travelled with his military family. He has an eclectic background with experience in Web development, retail customer service, and automotive repair. Aaron applied to the CarTech vocational school as a junior in high school and took night and weekend classes, simultaneously with high school classes, to start working toward an early automotive degree. He began learning a wide array of automotive specialty skills. While in high school, he rebuilt a classic car and fell in love with car rebuilding and restoration.

His vocational training landed him a summer job in an automotive repair and remodeling shop as an apprentice, learning hands-on welding and automotive parts sales, applying his passion for custom-modeled cars to his everyday job. His starting pay was $25 per hour. He will apply to colleges during his second year to obtain a four-year degree in engineering to complement his automotive repair studies.

Racing Operations Intern (Spring 2016: January - End of May) - Charlotte Motor Speedway (Concord, NC)

The Racing Operations Department is seeking candidates who are self-starting and able to multitask in a fast paced environment. Interns in this department need exceptional interpersonal and communication skills.

Responsibilities:
- Assist Director of Racing Operations in all aspects of on-track and competition racing operations. Including but not limited to:o Day-to-day staff management:
  - o Direct competition and related logistics
  - o Hiring/recruiting
  - o Jet Dryer logistics, staffing, and operations
  - o Oversee fence and wall repair or maintenance
  - o Oversee track repair
  - o Public Safety coordination with state and local authorities
  - o Training for officials and on-track crews
  - o Oversee the Track Services department
- Assist with management of all schedules for CMS events
- Help coordinate with NASCAR and other racing series for scheduling, logistics, race operations, and event management
- Assist with all Action Sports related entities
- Assist the CMS Events Department with events at CMS 1.5 mile track, the dirt track, and the zMAX Dragway.
- Assist with Summer Shootout and all US Legends operations with CMS
- Assist with all on-track racing activities
- Help facilitate safety and ground logistics with stunts for pre-race shows or press conferences
- Work directly with facility operations to ensure work orders from events and GS&L are prioritized and managed accordingly

CMS is one of the busiest facilities in the country and this internship will help with track rental customers. This is a hands on, fast paced internship. A lot of experience will be gained in event preparation and planning.

Intern must be able to work a minimum of 20 hours per week plus all events held during the semester.

Word and Excel Spreadsheet experience required.

This is an unpaid internship. As a token of gratitude, all interns who complete the semester internship and work the race events held during the semester internship will receive a stipend.

Note: When you apply for this job online, you will be required to answer the following questions:
1. Are you a college student or recent college graduate?
2. Write a personal statement in the space below. Include a description of the following: (1) your interest and experience in motorsports, (2) your background in sports management or related fields, (3) your educational background including the college courses that most interest you and (4) your motivations and goals for obtaining an internship with Charlotte Motor Speedway.
3. Do you understand this is an unpaid internship?
4. How did you hear about this program?
5. Are you over 21?

AARONSMITH
Automotive Repair

564 Constantine Road
Anaheim, CA 91913
C: 714.555.5555
aasmith@hotmail.com

CERTIFIED AUTOMOTIVE REPAIRER AND HOT ROD REBUILDER WITH CUSTOM FABRICATION EXPERTISE.

EXPERIENCE

Owner / Manager
Smith Website Design, Denver CO, 03/20xx – 10/20xx
Created a website design business as a solution for online presence for small and medium-sized businesses, civic clubs, organizations, and churches. Used cutting-edge technology including Macromedia Studio MX 2004, Dreamweaver, Flash, Fireworks, and FreeHand, as well as Graphic Design, Flash, JavaScript, CGI, CSS, HTML, and (X)HTML.

Custom Auto Body Technician / Mechanic
Hot Rod Shop, San Diego, CA, 05/20xx – 03/20xx
Built a 1970 Firebird. Assembled and dissembled the vehicle to the frame. Removed the old drive train and assembled a new motor, transmission, and wiring harness. Removed rusted sheet metal. Custom upholstered seats and door panels. Installed power windows.

OTHER
- Lived in Germany, Korea, Japan, and Bahrain. Traveled to more than 35 countries.
- Special Olympics, Germany, Group Leader for Bowling Tournament
- IT Skills: CISCO Networking I & II; LANs/WANs; MS Office Suite

EDUCATION

CarTech, Denver CO, 20xx
Certificate: Automotive Repair
Completed one year full-time program (120 credits) at the official technology school of the National Hot Rod Association.
- **Certified Automatic Transmission Rebuilder** (Licensed through 2017 / Automatic Transmission Rebuilder Association)
- **All Data Information Specialist**

Coursework in: Refrigerant Recovery & Recycling Review, Chassis and Drive Train Systems, Basic Engine Management Systems, Driveability Diagnostics, Race Team Technical Specialties

CarTech, Denver CO, 20xx
Certificate: Motorsports Chassis Foundation
Engaged in hands-instruction and internships specializing in metal working fabrication, and techniques including MIG and TIG frame design and modifications including boxing, tubular cross-members, c-notching, pro-street frame setup, roll cage construction, and complete tube chassis fabrication. Prepped for cutting, drilling, or machining using oxy-acetylene and plasma. Read and drew specialty mechanical drawings. Operated grinder and sanders. Applied attachment methods, metal finishing, and cutting.

CarTech, Denver CO, 20xx
Certificate: Street Rod Fabrication & Custom Painting with Automotive Technology
Customized vehicles and created works of art for street rods and custom fabrication. Used specialized sheet metal shaping fabrication techniques including chop tops, hidden pin hinges (suicide doors), and body construction including firewalls, floorboards, and transmission tunnels. Applied custom paint techniques including special effects, airbrushing, and pin striping as well as the application of specialized finishes.

Department of Defense General Adams High School, Wurzburg Germany, 20xx
- Attended Model United Nations Conference, The Hague
- Served on a team that designed and launched the school's website and was selected as the first-place winner in regional competition
- Varsity Football (Team Captain)

Pursuing an Aeronautics Internship

Calvin had some trouble in high school with dyslexia and needed special tutoring in reading and writing. But, he could perform highly complex repairs on cars and received high grades in technical courses. He was recognized with awards for his custom-built automobiles, including a1977 Porsche 930, 1976 FJ40 Four Wheeler, and the People's Choice Award for 1978 Chevy Truck. He received a full scholarship to the Commercial Aeronautics Program a community college. Today he is a Commercial Pilot.

Aeronautics Internship: Announcement

Time Commitment:
- Full-time minimum 40 hours per week (Monday–Friday)

Pay:
- $9.00 per hour

Education:
- Major in an aviation/aeronautical-based undergraduate degree program
- Minimum sophomore level
- Student must have an additional semester of classes remaining after completion of the internship
- Maintained 2.5 or above GPA

Experience:
- Participation in organizations and clubs desirable
- Proficient with Microsoft Office applications
- Database applications helpful, but not required

Skills and Abilities:
- Excellent communication (reading and writing), analytical and organizational skills
- Ability to manage time and multiple tasks effectively
- FAA Flight Certificates and ratings desirable

Personal Traits:
- Customer service oriented
- Self-motivated and energetic
- Team oriented
- Ability to work equally well alone or with others
- Flexibility to work in a dynamic, fast-paced environment
- Sense of humor

Job Duties:
- Projects include research, presentation, and meeting or involvement with or for Engineering, Hotels, Safety, Training, Dispatch, Scheduling, ATC, Navigation, or Chief Pilots (varies each term).

CALVIN **KLINE**

ckline101@com.com

2501B Wheaton Way
Davis, CA 90210
(970) 555-0000

CAREER GOAL

To enter an aeronautical program in college and gain relevant work experience toward my goal of becoming a commercial airline pilot.

TECHNICAL SKILLS

AUTOMOTIVE
Repair/restoration
Drive train/heating/AC
Diagnostics | Electrical
Rebuild and restore
Custom automobiles, | Four-wheelers
Award-winner

COMPUTER
Microsoft Office | Excel | Access

COMPETENCIES

Skilled analyst | problem-solver
Work independently and on teams
Self-motivated | Welcome challenge
Responsible | Detail-oriented
Multitask | Work hard,
Manage time effectively
Work well under pressure
Flexible in fast-paced environments

EDUCATION

La Quinta High School
Davis, CA: Class of 20xx
Completed Technical Program focusing on Industrial Design and Automotive Diagnostics and Repair. Courses included Industrial Physics, Welding, Machining, Drafting, Automotive Drive Train/Heating/AC, and Diagnostics and Electrical.

GPA 4.0 in all technical courses. Proven technical capabilities.

HONORS & AWARDS

Merit Awards in Welding and Automotive.
Received three-year full scholarship to AIMS Community College.
Won People's Choice Award in local 4 x 4 show for 1978 Chevy Truck.

CERTIFICATE PROGRAM

Aeronautical Certificate Candidate
Accepted into Commercial Aeronautics Program, AIMS Community College, Foresman, California. Beginning flight time.

EMPLOYMENT

Auto Technician
HIGHLINE MOTORS, Davis, CA—Summer 20xx
Install, repair, and maintain high-end import cars.

Craftsman
WOOD SHOP, Mead, CA—Summer 20xx
Crafted custom dashboards from quality hardwoods and veneers.

Autotech Trainee
WILF'S EUROPEAN MOTORS, Mead, CA—Summer 20xx

SPORTS/ SPECIAL INTERESTS

Purchase, repair, and sell custom-built automobiles.
Projects completed include a 1977 Porsche 930 and a 1976 FJ40 Four Wheeler—rebuilt and restored from the frame up.
Compete in local auto races.
Collect and ride dirt bikes.
High school sports included boxing and swim team.

Resume design concept by Molly Nix

COLLEGE ACCEPTANCE RESUME

This section will help you create a resume that you can send with your college application and use to apply for scholarships based on performance, grades, and experience. A resume for college acceptance needs to stand out from the other thousands of applicants that each college or university receives every year.

Your resume can also help you write your personal statement. When you have a record of your activities, honors, and courses, you can fill out the applications much faster. In addition, you can include a resume with your application package.

Pursuing a BA in Writing, Visual Information, and Media / Film

Cecile Callahan has been taking photographs, making videos, sculpting and creating art for years. She is passionate about film, photographs and has had her photographs in shows at her arts high school for peer review and competition. Cecile will be pursuing her interest in film-making, photography and humanitarian interests. Cecile is attending a small liberall arts college in Maryland.

CECILE callahan

110 Bryans Mill Road
Ellicott City, MD 21228
(123) 456 78 99
ccallahan1@gmail.com

Currently applying to enter a BA program in Cultural Anthropology with a focus on Visual Arts. Photographer, videographer, artist interested in cultural issues, history, women's rights, freedom of expression, the French language, and international travel. A finalist in several local film competitions for high school students, has exhibited and sold my artwork and photography, and is an AP Scholar.

Finalist in the Baltimore High School Film Festival

Art showcased in Row Home Lit, a literary magazine featuring art and writing from Baltimore County http://issuu.com Vol 1 2014

Created cover art for two novels

Created five short films on various subjects, uploaded to my YouTube channel

Finalist in the Garrison Forest High School Film Festival

EXPERIENCE

Intern
The Resume Place, Inc., Catonsville, MD
Jul 20xx – Aug 20xx
Jump-started The Resume Place's online client access database in Intuit Quickbase. Handle client phone calls, summarized/relayed important information, facilitated sales and service, and carried out small office tasks and administrative projects.

Community Service and Volunteer
- Assisted local artist Tom Chalkley with the completion of an arts-grant funded mural in the inner city of Baltimore, MD, July-July 20xx
- As a high school student, returned to Catonsville Middle School and assisted students, alongside an instructor, with the creation and publication of their literary magazine, 20xx – 20xx

Travel Experience
Dual citizenship (U.S. and UK). Traveled to England and France every year since one year of age; have made the journey solo each year since 12 years of age. Have also traveled to Spain, Ireland, and 16 U.S. states, visiting art museums at each destination.

EDUCATION

High School Diploma: Visual Arts, 20xx
George Washington Carver Center for Arts and Technology, Baltimore, MD
Cumulative High School GPA (weighted): 4.55
Specialized Courses: painting, drawing, photography and film (grades 9-12). Completing rigorous GT arts courses and AP college level Studio Arts course.

Extracurricular Activities
Film Society, 20xx – 20xx
Artemis Club (fundraising coordinator for local charities), 20xx – 20xx
Drumming Club, 20xx – 20xx

Honors
AP Scholar & National Art Honor Society, 20xx – 20xx

GT/AP Courses
GT English 9, 10; GT American Government 9 and World History 10; GT Biology 9 and Chemistry 10; GT Magnet Foundations of Art 9, GT Magnet; Drawing and Painting 10, GT Figure Drawing 11, and GT Interactive Media Production (Film-making) 10–12; AP English 1 (research paper: Gendered toys and their effect on young children), 12; AP US History 12; AP Studio Art 12

Resume template by Hloom.com

Pursuing a Degree in English Toward a Career in Marketing and Public Relations–Targeting a Career with Under Armour® Headquarters in Baltimore, MD

In high school, Tom didn't know what he wanted to pursue, until he heard about an internship opportunity with Under Amour®. He realized that he wanted to help market and develop public relations programs for the popular sports apparel products U.S.-wide. Tom did well writing for his high school newspaper. During his senior year, he was awarded a scholarship to the University of Maryland. He will major in English with a concentration in writing for marketing, publicity, and web content development for a future career with Under Armour®. He is applying for an internship, because it is well known that Under Armour® hires from their internship base. Often, the best way to break into a company is to start with part-time work or internships and move up with a targeted career in mind.

THOMAS GARNER

✉ garner@yahoo.com 📍 7290 Homewood Ct. College Park, MD 20740 📱 (410) 888-8098

EDUCATION

Tolbert Hall High School, Towson, Maryland
Expect to graduate in 20xx

ACADEMIC HONORS Peer Tutor (English Tutoring Program), McMullen Program (4-year honors program with culminating "thesis" style project). AP Courses (English, History). Top 10% of class. National Merit Scholar Honorable Mention.

ATHLETICS JV and Varsity Football; All MIAA Senior year Basketball and Rugby (Freshman/Sophomore) Nominee for "Scholar Athlete" for National Football Foundation (20xx)

ACTIVITIES Big Brothers Mentoring Program; French Club; Contributing Writer, School Newspaper

WORK EXPERIENCE

BANQUET SERVER **Martin's**, May 20xx–Present, Westminster, MD
- Provided hospitality service at special events held at major hotels in the Baltimore area.

LABORER **Sampson Concrete Co. Inc.**, June 20xx–Aug 20xx
- Worked 65- to 80-hour weeks doing concrete construction in and around the Baltimore area.
- Learned various construction techniques including some carpentry and masonry skills.

SEASONAL TEAMMATE **Active Pick, Manifest (weekends)**, Baltimore, MD Summer 20xx
- Received product from inbound freight trucks; utilize hand-held computers for product inventory database; reviews barcodes; trained in and use a pallet jack for storage of received merchandise. Developed efficient space planning for inventory storage. Created labeling of customer product. Controlled quality and quantity of the order.

ACADEMIC GOAL

To attend a college or university with a strong English or Public Relations program and to pursue internships in public relations.

CORE SKILLS

Writing

Oral Communications

Presentation Development and Delivery

Research and Critical-Thinking

Customer Service

Microsoft Office

French

ADDITIONAL SKILLS

Adobe Acrobat, ACT! 2000
FDP Contact Partner
Lexis-Nexis, Factiva
Bacons/Cision
Google AdWords
Yahoo! Sponsored Search
Omniture; Experience with QDA Miner
Smart Office 5
Adobe Photoshop Elements 5.0.

Pursuing a Degree in Business

Matthew Manowitz had this to say about his future plans: "My school and summer activities and my part-time job revolve around golf. I love the game, the people, and the business. I hope someday to be involved in the golf industry in sales, management, or some other aspect of the sport. I would like to continue to play golf in college. I am sending my resume directly to golf coaches for their review. I know I must be realistic, though, because landing a spot on a college golf team is very competitive. My top priority, really, is to gain admission to a college with a strong business program."

Matthew Manowitz

ACADEMIC GOAL

To attend a college or university with a strong **Business Administration** program focusing on International Business.

ATHLETIC GOAL

To utilize my experience and strong background in competitive junior golf to become a member of a college/university golf team.

SKILLS SUMMARY

Articulate and responsible
Proficient in Word and PowerPoint
Enthusiastic team player
Enjoy new challenges
Excellent public speaking skills
Strong interpersonal skills

EDUCATION

Mount St. Joseph High School, Baltimore, Maryland
Junior; expect to graduate May 20xx
College Preparatory Classes—Full honors curriculum 20xx to 20xx. Courses include French II & III, Chemistry, Geometry, Language Arts, and World History.

GOLF ACHIEVEMENTS

More than five years of experience competing in area junior golf in tournaments, including two years in the Titleist Junior Tour, PGA Middle Atlantic Section. Experienced in stroke play and match play. Current USGA Handicap: 7.9. Lowest 18-hole score: 74. Average 18-hole score: 80.

- Sophomore Year, 20xx–20xx
  Varsity Golf Team, position 5/6 on a 10-man team.

- Freshman Year, 20xx–20xx
  JV Golf Team, position 2/3 on a 7-man team. MIAA Champions, 20xx.

OTHER SPORTS/ EXTRACURRICULAR ACTIVITIES

- Junior Varsity Track Team, 2 years
- Recreational Team Basketball, 6 years
- Volunteer Coach for youth basketball program, 2 years

EMPLOYMENT

Caddy & Bag Room Assistant
Hunt Valley Golf Club, Ellicott City, Maryland
Summers 20xx & 20xx

25065 Triadelphia Mill Road Ellicott City, MD 21117   manowitz@net.net   (410) 444-3333

Pursuing a Degree in International Affairs and Environmental Awareness

Molly Jackson believes in making a difference. Her exceptional academic ability has provided her with opportunities to share her interest in different cultures with travels as a People to People Ambassador. Her four years (since eighth grade) taking Japanese as a foreign-language elective were very beneficial. Although she is not totally fluent, her attempt and desire to communicate brought smiles to many faces as she spent time with the people of Japan.

Not only does Molly excel academically, but she has also demonstrated her leadership in both the athletic and volunteer arenas. As an avid swimmer, she has successfully coached many young children over the past two years in her job as an assistant swim coach. During the school year she has served as president of the Environmental Club and as an Ambassador internationally as well as locally within her school. Perhaps most notable is her selection to the Athletic Leadership Council, which promotes good sportsmanship, integrity on and off the field, commitment, and teamwork.

Molly also loves art. She participated in an internship program allowing her to experience firsthand the world of work. Serving as an assistant photographer and preparing educational materials at the nature center were great opportunities. Her role as an ambassador, internships, volunteer activities, and work experiences along with her academic achievements will serve her well as she pursues her college search.

MOLLY R. JACKSON

mollyrjackson@email.com

8637 Burkhall St.
Atlanta, GA 30308

404-555-1212 (Home)
404-555-0000 (Cell)

Profile

Outstanding student with a broad range of talents and interests. Enthusiastic and passionate about greater social and environmental awareness. Chosen to travel to Japan and Australia with an international cultural exchange program. Award-winning scholar, artist, and athlete; recognized by teachers and peers as a true leader. Self-motivated, hands-on attitude with excellent interpersonal skills.

Education

Parker High School; Atlanta, Georgia
High School Diploma
International Baccalaureate Certificate Candidate
Notable Courses:

GPA: 96% (Numeric Average)
Graduation expected June 20xx

- AP Calculus AB
- AP Statistics
- AP Environmental Science
- AP U.S. History
- AP World History
- AP 3-D Design
- AP Psychology
- IB 20th Century History
- IB English

Experience

Max Roland Professional Photographer; Atlanta, Georgia   08/20xx–Present
Intern—Senior Year
   Assist photographer with photo shoots, editing of images, and creation of photo albums.

Chattahoochee National Recreational Area; Atlanta, Georgia   08/20xx–12/20xx
Intern—Junior Year
   Prepared and supported development of educational materials for school groups and individuals; assisted instructors as needed.

Beaches Aquatic Club; Atlanta, Georgia   Summer 20xx/Summer 20xx
Assistant Swim Coach
   Planned, organized, and conducted practice sessions for 120 swimmers ages 4–18, twice a day, 5 days a week; provided training, instruction on performance principles, and motivation.

Awards and Honors

Academics/Leadership/Community

- People to People International Ambassador ▪ Interact Club ▪ President—Environmental Club
- Parker High Ambassador ▪ Columbia College Scholar ▪ Erskine Fellow Award
- Northeastern Book Award ▪ Wofford Scholar ▪ Principal's Scholar Award

Athletics/Leadership in Sports

- Athletic Leadership Council ▪ Varsity Swimming Achievement Award
- Most Valuable Swimmer (Varsity Girls) ▪ Most Valuable Defense Player (Varsity Lacrosse)

INTERNSHIP RESUME

Many corporations, small businesses, and government agencies offer 6- to 12-week summer internships or year-round internships with flexible hours to students who are 16 years or older, are enrolled in high school full time, and have GPAs of 2.5 or higher.

Some internship opportunities are paid; however, some are unpaid. An internship can give you hands-on experience in a certain industry that you might be interested in.

High School Student Seeking Literary Internship – Internship Announcement for Marketing Writer

Description:
We are currently looking for virtual interns who can write articles and persuasive web copy daily that will engage our readers and make them take the necessary action required of them.

In return you will gain valuable experience in research using online methods on how to write different kinds of web copy geared towards different kinds of audiences.

Remember this is an unpaid virtual internship and can be done from any location in the world. All you need is a reliable computer and stable internet connection.

If you are interested in this position send your resume,a short cover letter and some samples of your writing.

Responsibilities: Writing articles, newsletters, press releases, ebooks, blog posts and rewriting private label rights content with your own voice to make it unique.

Requirements:
- Skills in English, Creative Writing, Journalism, Mass Communication
- Internet savvy
- Familiar with WordPress blogging platform
- Excellent grammar and spelling
- Creativity
- Attention to detail

Position: Part-time, Unpaid

Emily K. Thomspon

43 Village Court , Westboro, MD 00000
Phone: (000) 555-5555   E-Mail: ekthompson@gmail.com

Education

Westboro High School, Westboro MD   **Expect to graduate May 20xx**

Academic Honors:
Honor Roll, average GPA 3.8/4.0, 20xx–present
Advanced Placement: U.S. History and English coursework
Activities:
Editor-in-Chief, *Phoenix Literary Arts Magazine,* 20xx–20xx
Maryland State Forensics League, President
　　　Debate National Competitor: Kansas City, KS (20xx); Milwaukee, WI (20xx);
　　　Detroit, MI (20xx)
Dramatic Theater: *Twelve Angry Jurors; Flowers for Algernon;* and leading role in
　　　You Can't Take It with You

Workshops

Hawaiian Language and Culture, Maui Community College, Maui, HI, Fall 20xx
Writing and Thinking, Lewis College, Seattle, WA, Summer 20xx
National Outdoor Leadership School, Lander, WY, Summer 20xx
Andre Brougher (*Homicide* series) Shakespeare Workshop, Winter 20xx
Writer's Workshop, State University, Frederick, MD, Summer 20xx

Honors and Recognition

Winner of Redmond College's "Women Writing about Women" Competition,
April 20xx, one of three selected out of 140 portfolios entered

Published Poetry

Salt of the Earth literary magazine
Singing Sands Review
The Apprentice Writer
Featured reader in publicized Fells Point and Baltimore poetry readings

Experience

Internship, Haleakala National Park, Maui, HI   **Sep – Dec 20xx**
Interpretation and special projects. Guide and interpreter for 20-minute presentations daily.

Teacher's Aide, Newton Elementary School, Baltimore, MD   Spring 20xx

References

Karol Porter, English Chair, Westboro High School, (401) 333-3333, kporter@westborohs.edu

Resume created with Microsoft Word Project Template

JOB RESUME

A good resume makes looking for work so much easier. Many employers are impressed by high school students and first-time jobseekers who have strong resumes. To apply for a job, you should email or hand-deliver your resume and cover letter to the employer. You should highlight your previous work experience in a resume, but the rest of your education information is important as well.

In addition, you should include a cover letter in order to introduce yourself. A cover letter is a way to tell more about yourself beyond what a person can see from your resume. It should be professional, but not too stiff. You can simply write your cover letter in the email and attach your resume if you are applying via email. If you're applying on an online application system, you should upload both a cover letter and a resume.

Applying for Job in Construction

Ron Milestone volunteered one year to be a coordinator for the construction projects for the local community. This was the beginning of his future career. Ron's paid positions involved lifeguarding and teaching children to swim, but he found that he enjoyed working with his hands and supervising projects. He continued to work with the construction committee and was successful in recruiting carpenters, electricians, sheetrock experts, painters, and other construction specialists to repair and upgrade various properties in the area. "I felt inspired to help people with improving the quality of their homes and businesses," he said.

Job Announcement

Job Category - Construction - Management
Education Required - College Degree Not Required
Job Type - Full Time

The Assistant Construction Manager will assist in the supervision of all on-site construction, including the scheduling of subcontractors on the job, resolving day-to-day problems on the job site, and inspecting all work during construction to ensure compliance with plans and specifications. Some construction experience is required.

Essential responsibilities of an Assistant Construction Manager include obtaining all permits necessary to construct houses, ordering all materials required to construct houses, and working with the Construction Manager and Project Manager to set up and monitor the construction schedule.

This is an excellent opportunity to join one of the nation's most respected Fortune 1000 companies!

Qualifications:
We seek an Assistant Construction Manager experienced in residential construction management who has strong organizational and people skills in addition to sound knowledge of production homebuilding.

If you meet these requirements, and you enjoy working in a fast-paced, team-oriented environment, this may be the opportunity for you!

This position offers an excellent compensation and benefits package, including comprehensive medical/dental, 401(k) with a company match, discounted stock purchase, discounts on mortgages, homes, appliances, and much more!

RONALD MILESTONE

1456 E. Marion Street Baltimore, MD 21204
Cell 433.333.3333 | milestone789@mail.com

EDUCATION

Expected Graduation: 20xx

TOWSON CATHOLIC HIGH SCHOOL
Towson, MD

WORK EXPERIENCE

THE PARSON CONTRACTING COMPANY

Baltimore, MD
Summer 20xx

PROJECT ENGINEER INTERN / ASSISTANT
Worked as an assistant to a project engineer on a $55M construction project to build a visitor's center and underground parking garage.

- Interfaced daily with contractors, engineers, and other construction support professionals to review project status. Completed invoices and other administrative paperwork.
- Wrote and presented status reports at weekly project managers' meetings.
- Enhanced skills in problem resolution, project management, and cost management.

PARK SWIM CLUB

Towson, MD
Summer 20xx

MANAGER
Promoted to manager within two weeks. Supervised 17 lifeguards. Developed weekly work schedules for all employees. Maintained safe environment for patrons by enforcing club rules and regulations.

- Learned to effectively mediate and satisfy customer concerns.
- Acquired leadership and crew management skills.
- Selected as Lifeguard of the Year.

HAWAII PARK CENTER

Honolulu, HI
January 20xx to January 20xx

LIFEGUARD
Performed and assisted with water rescue and situations. Patrolled the harbor. Performed beach maintenance. Received Aloha award for customer service.

ACTIVITIES / VOLUNTEERING

September 20xx to Present

HABITAT FOR HUMANITY
Participated in community service construction projects.

January 20xx to Present

SALVATION ARMY
Perform community service helping to sort and process donations.

SKILLS

Knowledge of construction principles, basic building systems, and project management

Resume template by Hloom.com

Sous Chef Seeking Sales Position

Ryan Abel has achieved success as a sous chef and has learned how to buy food, products, wine, and beer. He knows how to negotiate with vendors and to select the best products for his changing menu at the County Cork Wine Pub. But Ryan was tired of the long hours, weekends, events, and hard labor of cooking and preparation. He decided he wanted to represent an upscale food distributor, manage events, consult with restaurant owners and chefs, and hopefully make more money. He has used his degree in Biotechnology as a Sous Chef, recognizing the importance of ingredients for quality menus and recipes. His new resume features his various skills and experience in the restaurant industry.

Job Announcement

We are looking for an exceptionally talented Sales Representative who will thrive in a fast-paced, challenging, and dynamic work environment, and most importantly, is someone who loves to have fun. Our ideal candidate is someone whose entrepreneurial spirit and passion for beer, sports, health, and fitness is contagious.

Job Responsibilities
- Understanding and embracing Three Notch'd's mission, purpose, vision, and strategy, while engaging wholesale and retail customers with it.
- Organizing and executing events at accounts and in the market including beer dinners, tap takeovers, festivals, tasting events, and samplings.
- Achieving various sales, marketing, and MBO goals.
- Keeping a daily tracker of sales goals and account calls.
- Executing distributor work-withs and sales performance initiatives.

Job Requirements
- 1-2 year of sales experience is required.
- Ability to work some weeknights and weekends for various events and promotions.
- A valid driver's license and a clean driving record is a must.
- Must have access to a personal vehicle.
- Applicant should be driven, able to multitask, and competitive.
- Proficiency in Microsoft Office (Word, Excel, Powerpoint, Outlook).

Physical Requirements
Candidate should be willing and able to lift at least 31.5 pounds.

Ryan Abel

Permanent Address: 1912 McCutchin Dr. • Montego Bay, MD 21834
Cell : 555-555-5555 • Email: rmabel1988@gmail.com
Targeting Entry-Level Position

- Quickly learn and master new technology; equally successful in both team and self-directed settings
- High knowledge of laboratory techniques and quick learner of new hardware and procedures
- Proficient in Microsoft Word, Excell, Powerpoint, SPSS software, BLAST, ArcMap Softwares
- Great public speaker through the presentation of my research
- Personable, outgoing, easy to talk to

EDUCATION

JAMES MADISON UNIVERSITY
 BIOTECHNOLOGY   20xx - 20xx

EXPERIENCE

County Wine Pub   June 20xx – Present

- I have spent the past year working at The County Cork Wine Pub, working in the food industry has allowed me to appreciate flavor profiles; also having given me many opportunities to sample multiple types of beers through liquor reps. As well as utilizing beer in recipes, order to create food pairings.

Pink Flamingo Snowball Stand   June 20xx – June 20xx

- Manager of local snowball stand to receive products, track inventory, and provide customer service.

Jolly Pig Food Truck Operator   May 20xx – June 20xx

- Prepared and served food.

Pool Chemical Operator and Assistant Manager   20xx – 20xx

- Balanced and maintained pool chemicals, kept stock records of chemicals, kept daiy logs of chemical readings. Managed a team of 15 lifeguards

JMU SIFE   20xx - Present

- Member of JMU Students in Free Enterprise; active in community service

1912 McCutchin Dr. • Montego Bay, MD 21834 • Email: rmabel1988@gmail.com • Cell : 555-555-5555

RYAN ABEL

WORK EXPERIENCE

PROFILE

Personable and professional sous chef at a local upscale wine pub. Experience in management and sales. Able to work well with customers and coworkers.

EDUCATION

Bachelor of Arts
Biotechnology
James Madison University
May 2013

SOUS CHEF • *County Cork Wine Pub* • *Jonesville, MD* • *June 20xx – present*

Assist and support executive chef in overseeing kitchen operations for this local wine pub. Prepare menus with the owner and the executive chef in order to provide customers with exciting seasonal menu options. Train new kitchen staff on recipe preparation and safe food handling. Act as kitchen manager when manager is out, assigning duties and ensuring that food is prepared efficiently and effectively. Market new menu options to new and returning customers, providing detailed explanations of all options. Maintain in-depth and current knowledge of all menu items.

Key Accomplishments:
- Perform monthly inventory checks in order to ensure proper tracking of goods within the restaurant.
- Worked with Flying Dog Brewery and the executive chef in order to prepare a menu for two beer tastings. Created the menu to pair food with over 5 different types of beer and marketed the event to our current customers.
- After realizing that customers wanted locally grown produce, reached out to a local farm to provide produce to The Cork. Proposed new supplier to the owner, who agreed. This past year, the farm was able to provide fresh, local produce to the restaurant while resulting in savings to the owner as compared to the previous supplier.

MANAGER • *Pink Flamingo Snowball Stand* • *Montego Bay, MD* • *June 20xx – June 20xx*

As manager for a local snowball stand, oversaw up to 10 employees at a time. Performed inventory to ensure proper tracking of products, notifying owners what supplies needed to be ordered. Provided excellent customer service to customers and their families. Managed multiple tasks in order to quickly deliver goods to customers. Worked with wholesale distributors to pick up orders. Marketed new products to customers and made suggestions to owners regarding the best marketing strategies.

OPERATOR • *Jolly Pig Food Truck* • *May 20xx – June 20xx*

Prepared and served food in fast-paced environment. Interacted with, served, and cashed out customers. Informed customers about pricing and information for catering and private parties

POOL CHEMICAL OPERATOR AND ASSISTANT MANAGER • *Freedom Swim Club* • *Jonesville, MD* • *20xx - 20xx*

Balanced and maintained pool chemicals, kept stock records of chemicals, kept daily logs of chemical readings. Managed a team of 15 lifeguards, including ensuring coverage for all shifts and resolving scheduling conflicts.

3/9/20xx

Ryan Abel
1912 McCutchin Dr.
Montego Bay, MD 21834

Dear Scott:

As soon as I was referred to you by my friend Kelvin Birch, who works in your Harrisonburg location, I was immediately interested. For the past two years, I have been working in an upscale wine pub, providing clients and customers with a personable and enjoyable dining experience. During my tenure as a cook, I have learned many aspects of the restaurant industry, and have learned a lot about customer service and working in a fast-paced environment. I believe my restaurant kitchen experience will add to your company's team and overall success in expanding your market.

Once a month at my current job, we put together a wine tasting, pairing wines with small plates of food, and have also done similar tastings with various area microbreweries. My experience with the preparation of these menus would prove to be an advantage while selling and distributing Three Notch'd beer. In addition, as a graduate of JMU, I am familiar with the Northern Virginia area and am confident I could help Three Notch'd gain new clients.

I believe that my skill sets would strengthen the Three Notch'd Brewing Company, and I would love an opportunity to work and grow with the company.

Thank you very much for your time and consideration.

Yours truly,

Ryan Abel

High School Student Seeking Position at Upscale Grocery Store

Justin Mack was looking for a position suitable for a high school student, and when Whole Foods moved into the neighborhood, Justin wanted to apply for a position there. Justin highlighted his academic achievements, volunteer experience, part time work, and reasons why he thought he was a good fit for the company.

Job Announcement - Whole Foods Grocery Service Team Member

As a member of our Grocery Team, your role will include receiving and preparing product, maintaining the Grocery floor and displays, and selling product in support of regional Grocery standards. You will ensure a positive company image by providing courteous, friendly, and efficient customer service to customers and team members.

DUTIES:
- Give every customer immediate and undivided attention. Surprise and delight the customers with consistent, delicious food.
- Ensure a fresh and appealing display by keeping cases and shelves clean and well stocked by front-facing, checking codes, rotating, and removing out-of-date products.
- Maintain accurate department signage and pricing.
- Stock and clean grocery shelves, bulk bins, frozen and dairy case.
- Maintain back stock in good order.
- Keep Grocery department clean, sweep floors and maintain sweep logs.
- Assist with sampling program, keeping sample areas full, clean, and appealing.
- Follow and comply with all applicable health and sanitation procedures and adhere to safe work practices.
- Operate and sanitize all Grocery equipment in a safe and proper manner.
- This job posting is intended to describe the general requirements for the performance of this job. It is not a complete statement of duties, responsibilities or requirements. Other duties not listed here may be assigned by leadership.

REQUIREMENTS:
- Previous Grocery experience preferred.
- Excellent communication skills and willingness to work as part of a team; ability to communicate effectively with customers.
- Ability to follow instructions and procedures.
- Ability to sell proactively.
- Ability to learn basic knowledge of all products carried in department.
- Effective time management skills.
- Strong work ethic and integrity.
- Ability to visually examine products for quality and freshness.
- Ability to work in a wet and cold environment.
- Available for flexible scheduling to meet the needs of the department.
- Use of box cutters.
- Use of electric pallet jacks or other heavy machinery.

Essential Job Functions:
- Stand and walk for extended periods of time.
- Bend and stoop to grasp objects and climb ladders. Bend and twist neck and waist, reach above and below shoulders and squat.
- Bend and lift loads, not to exceed 50 pounds. Push and pull carts weighing up to 100 pounds.
- Repetitive use of hands for grasping, pushing, pulling, and fine manipulation.
- Environmental exposure to extreme temperatures (coolers, ovens, freezer, outdoors, etc.)

Justin Mack

CONTACT

4758 Fox Hill Road
Ashburn, VA 20006

jmack4758@gmail.com

(703) 555-5555 (h)
(703) 666-6666 (c)

LANGUAGES

ENGLISH

GERMAN

SKILLS

MICROSOFT OFFICE

ADOBE PHOTOSHOP

ADOBE PRESENTER

ADOBE ILLUSTRATOR

HOBBIES

WHY HIRE ME

As a rising high school sophomore, I will be around for at least three years, making the effort to train me worthwhile.

My academic and personal achievements demonstrate dependability, maturity, desire to help others, and the ability to learn and solve problems quickly.

I am able to listen carefully, follow directions, and be responsive to others' needs.

I live in the community just a few blocks from the store, so I understand the clientele and will not have transportation issues.

I am raising money to continue my missions work with Open Arms International in Brazil, which I am extremely passionate about.

EXPERIENCE

Resume Place Social Media Coordinator
2014 - present; up to 5 hours per week
Update and post federal job search information on LinkedIn, Facebook and Twitter. Edit and advise on Resume Place website. Consult with developmental editing for *Creating Your First Resume.* Update email marketing database.

Brazil Missions Trip, Spring Break 2015
Part of highly effective team that conducted a Vacation Bible School for over 200 children at the Terena Indian Reservation in Aquiduana, Brazil. Served as team lead for efficient preparation, organization, distribution, and clean up of snacks for camp participants for two camp sessions each day. Accompanied worship songs on drum and cajon. Successfully communicated with Indian children throughout the week despite language barriers. Learned the joy and value of serving others.

Volunteering
Participate in a variety of volunteer opportunities to assist others in our community:
- Bring and serve food at the Loudoun Homeless Shelter
- Work with elementary school students at Vacation Bible School
- Assist with activities at community fundraiser to raise money for childhood cancer
- Coach elementary school children in basketball

ACHIEVEMENTS

Gifted Program (ability to learn quickly and solve problems)

Honor Roll (all years, consistency in working hard)

Technology Student of the Year (2014, able to work with hands and solve problems)

School Safe Ambassador (selected for excellence in leading others and communication on difficult issues)

EDUCATION

Riverside High School, Lansdowne, VA
Expected graduation - 2018
All honors / AP courses, 4.15 GPA

MILITARY RESUME

If you are interested in applying to a military academy or becoming involved in an ROTC program in college, you may want to think about creating a Military Resume. The military service typically looks favorably on those who hold leadership roles, are involved in community and civic affairs, and have some athletic ability. The best time to apply to the military academies or to ROTC programs is during the spring of your junior year in high school.

Military Family Member Applying for Electrical Systems Specialist with U.S. Air Force

Nathan Brown is an Air Force family member, and the military is in his blood. He will be applying to the USAF. His Air Force Recruiter could see Nathan's strong military experience, JROTC experience, and areas of interest. The recruiter said that, with his interest and background in computer repair and electronics, Nathan could be trained for the Electrical Systems Specialist Military Occupation within the USAF.

Job Announcement - U.S. Air Force Electrical Systems Specialist

Air Force Electrical Systems Specialist Career Description
Every Air Force base and installation around the world is like a city unto itself—and every city requires electricity. It is a fundamental utility that allows our command centers and Airmen to successfully fulfill their missions. Installing, repairing and maintaining this electrical network is the job of the Electrical Systems specialists. Imagine if our space command couldn't communicate with our satellites or if our hospitals couldn't operate their lifesaving equipment, and you begin to see just how vital this career is to the Air Force.

Career Tasks
- Install, service, modify and repair electrical equipment and systems
- Troubleshoot and repair electrical and industrial electronic circuits and equipment
- Repair and restore service to failed overhead and underground electrical systems
- Climb poles to the height of 40 feet using gaffs
- Install, maintain and repair overhead distribution systems required for Air Force Service Code (AFSC) award
- Install and maintain airfield lighting systems as well as other specialized electrical systems

Relevant Interests & Skills
Mechanics, Electronics, Maintenance and Repair, Problem-solving, Science

Training
After eight and a half weeks of Basic Military Training, every Airman goes to technical training to learn their career. Here's the basic information about Electrical Systems technical training:
School location: Sheppard AFB [TX]
Length of course: 99 days
College degree earned: Mechanical and Electrical Technology
College credits earned: 36

Ramstein Air Base | APO AE 09094
(0049) 06371-1459475
brownn101@aol.com

NATHAN T. BROWN

OBJECTIVE

To join the U.S. Air Force as a military professional

SKILLS SUMMARY

Analytical skills
Schematic readings and manuals
Computer repair, networking, security setup
Strong technical and diagnostic skills
Leadership and communications skills
Keyboarding skills: 40 wpm

EDUCATION

Ramstein High School, Ramstein Air Base, Germany, Class of 20xx

Activities:
- JROTC Member; recognized for leadership and outstanding attendance award
- Junior Reserve Officer Training
- Member, Wrestling Team, 20xx to present
- Corps Drill Team

Area of Focus: Computer Technology Courses
- Computer Service and Repair
- Technology Learning Community
- CISCO Certification and Training
- Other coursework included building and troubleshooting computers; studying Windows; installing software

Honors & Awards:
- Merit Awards in Intro to Computer and Windows Vista Course

EMPLOYMENT

Computer Repair, Freelance, Ramstein Air Base and Vogelweh Housing Area, 20xx to present. Hourly, $8.00
Troubleshoot, repair and assist with training in Windows, Word, and email programs.

Electronics Set-Up Assistant, Ramstein Air Base, Civil Engineering, Summer 20xx. Hourly: $8.00
Grounds maintenance, event set-up, electronic equipment set-up.

ACTIVITIES

Summer Camp Counselor, The Ramstein Community Center, Ramstein Air Base, summer 20xx. Planned activities and crafts for children ages 6 to 12 in small groups.

LANGUAGES & TRAVEL

Speak German moderately. Traveled throughout Europe for four years during summers and holidays. Experienced with cross-cultural environments. Enjoy military history and war-game scenarios and simulation systems. Member of the Ramstein Southside Fitness Center.

Seth had been working at Kentucky Fried Chicken for seven years and was stuck in the fast food industry. He finally decided to meet with an Air National Guard recruiter and come up with a plan to utilize the skills he picked up at Kentucky Fried Chicken: computers, maintenance of equipment, quality control, and manufacturing. The recruiter recognized that Seth is a hard worker, having received four "World Famous" pins for hard work and teamwork. These are qualities that the Air National Guard will need to repair aircraft control surfaces. Seth now has a new career and will continue with the Air National Guard both as a Regular Guard and on deployments if activated. He will receive new training and certifications to improve his career objectives in the Air National Guard.

About the Air National Guard, 175th Wing

The 175th Wing, located in Baltimore, Maryland, has a dual mission: to augment active duty forces, and to assist State authorities during civil and natural disaster emergencies. The A-10 Thunderbolt has missions involving close air support, forward air control, combat search and rescue, and night flying operations in either an offensive or defensive capacity.

Maryland Air National Guard Benefits

◆ EDUCATION BENEFITS: Maryland Air Guard members can get up to 100% tuition assistance at state colleges and universities.
◆ MEDICAL BENEFITS: Maryland Air Guard members and their families get low-cost health insurance and life insurance.

SETH BELL

597 Breakstone Drive • Youngstown, MD 21844
Home: 410-555-5555 • Cell: 443-555-5555 • Email: sethbell@gmail.com

SKILLS

- General: Good worker, able to work well on teams, follow directions and take the initiative. Cooperative with positive attitude, able to pay attention to details.
- Writing: Skilled in writing composition, spelling, grammar use and proofreading.
- Computer: MS Word, MS Paint; Internet; e-mail; AutoCAD; programming experience with Java; programming experience with Python
- Music: Skilled in guitar, bass, moderate piano, moderate drums, composition, performance, creativity.

EDUCATION

Undergraduate Studies, music major, Carroll Community College, Westminster, MD, 20xx-20xx; 61 credits; GPA: 3.5 computer science major, University of Maryland, Baltimore County, Baltimore, MD; 102.5 credits to date;

Diploma, Century High School, Eldersburg, MD; June 20xx

A.A degree, Carroll Community College, Westminster, MD; May 20xx

Special Project: Designed and painted mural for Sykesville Middle School. Planned and created draft small-scale version; transferred larger scale to wall. Outlined and painted design.

WORK EXPERIENCE

Food Service Associate   Aug. 20xx – March 20xx
Kentucky Fried Chicken   Eldersburg, MD

- Customer Service: Served customers, preparing and packaging orders to specifications. Resolved customer problems, ensuring satisfaction.
- Food Preparation: Cooked and prepared range of foods, quickly and accurately filling customer orders. Washed dishes and cleaned food prep and cooking areas. Followed all applicable health and sanitation standards. Properly stored food in designated containers; verified freshness of product before serving. Informed supervisors when supplies were low or equipment was not working properly. As needed, completed kitchen closing duties.
  - *Accomplishment:* Recognized for teamwork and effort: received four "World Famous" pins.

Busser   Jan. 20xx – May 20xx
Osaka Hibachi Grill   Eldersburg, MD

- Server Support: Cleared, cleaned and reset tables for servers. Took dishes to kitchen; assisted dishwasher as needed. Cleaned up spills, swept and emptied trash. Performed serving, cleaning and stocking duties to facilitate customer service. Ran errands for waitstaff and responded to customer requests. Set up restaurant before opening and performed closing duties.

Field Marketer   Oct. 20xx – March 20xx
Pinnacle Energy Incorporated   Elkridge, MD

- <u>Representative:</u> Responsible for articulating products and services. Established appointments with residential costumers. Promoted to Team Leader, which included transporting, supervising, and navigating field marketers.

- <u>Abilities and skills included:</u>
  - Ability to record accurate measurements and translate measurements into a visual layout and scope of work to be performed.
  - Skills to organize and follow through in handling details, documentation, records, requests, and processes.
  - Ability to self-manage time and activities to meet deadlines, goals, quotas, and customer requirements.

VOLUNTEER WORK

Mission Trip to Poland, 20xx ~ Soap Boxing Factory, (boxed soap for poor), 20xx-xx ~
Mission Trip to Virginia, 20xx ~ Rouse Company Yearly Volunteer Day, 20xx-xx ~
Summer Stretch (community service), 8 weeks, 20xx, 20xx

Seth Bell
597 Breakstone Drive
Youngstown, MD 21884
(999) 888-8888
October 25, 20xx

Federal Human Resources Recruiter
Defense Finance and Accounting Service
3333 Milton Ave.
Cleveland, OH, 90999

Dear Human Resources Recruiter:

Please find enclosed my federal resume, DD-214 and performance evaluation for the position of **Accounting Technician, GS-0515-7**.

My relevant qualifications include:
- Two years of experience as an Aircraft Armament Systems Craftsman. As a Craftsman, I have general competencies that will support my skill as an Accounting Technician.
- As an Structural Maintenance professional, I controlled supplies and maintenance equipment for maximum readiness and ensured safety of 3,000 pieces of equipment.

I would be an asset to your organization because:
- My ability to work well with others is proven. I have been a team member in my military and civilian work experiences.
- I have been recognized for my skill in reconciling complex issues with inventory control for flight line personnel to ensure readiness of operations.

I would like to apply my experience to an entry-level position with DFAS, the largest accounting firm in the world. Thank you for your time and consideration.

Sincerely,

Seth Bell

Enclosures: Federal Resume, DD-214 and transcript

FEDERAL STUDENT JOBS RESUME

The federal job market is significantly different from the private sector. Federal resumes are more detailed and complex to prepare and a response to your federal application can take months. If you're applying to the federal government either for an internship or for a competitive service position, it is critical that your applications are laser-focused on what each federal position demands. The federal government uses its most popular internship program, Pathways, to hire most of the students who currently work for the federal government.

Applying for Civil Engineer Position with the Federal Government

Ashley is from a family of engineers. Her father and brothers are mechanical and general engineers. She is interested in Civil Engineering and would like to pursue a stable position in the government. She is emphasizing her engineering coursework and projects during her degree program in Civil / Environmental Engineering. In her resume, she included examples of teamwork, research projects, life-cycle analysis, and all of her mathematics courses.

JOB ANNOUNCEMENT

Civil Engineer
The primary duties of the Civil Engineer includes creating detailed designs of water and wastewater treatment systems as well as collection systems under instruction from the Project Engineer. More specific responsibilities include preparing plans for water and wastewater systems writing specifications analysis and study-level reports for water and wastewater treatment distribution and collection systems determining appropriate design methods equipment sizing and selection and working directly with the owner. Conducts quality control reviews of completed designs. Should be familiar with water and wastewater treatment processes and technologies.

Qualifications
BS/MS in Civil or Environmental Engineering. Interest or experience designing water/wastewater treatment facilities. Microsoft Office experience required. Must be able to work in a team environment. An attitude and commitment to being an active participant of our employee-owned culture is a must.

Primary Location: United States-Hawaii-Honolulu
Industry: Water Treatment
Schedule: Full-time
Employee Status: Regular
Business Class: WW Treatment and Effluent Mgmt - 006

ASHLEY HUI
1234 Nehoa Street Honolulu, HI 96822
Phone: 555-256-2882
Email: Ashley.Hui19@gmail.com
United States Citizen

EDUCATION

BACHELOR OF SCIENCE, Civil/Environmental Engineering; University of Hawaii at Manoa
Honolulu, HI USA – 08/20xx - 12/20xx; GPA: 3.77 out of 4.0
- Manoa Service Learning Award Scholarship
- American Society of Civil Engineers
- Chair of Activities Committee for ASCE, Pacific Southwest Conference

KNOWLEDGE OF ENGINEERING PRINCIPLES, CONCEPTS AND THEORIES. Developed knowledge, skills, and abilities with regard to the practice of sustainable civil and environmental engineering, including substantial exposure to applied mechanics, structural analysis and design, hydraulics, surveying, surveying and traffic engineering. **Specific relevant classes include**: Physics, Chemistry, Calculus, Applied Mechanics, and Thermo Dynamics.

MAJOR RESEARCH PAPER on Construction Materials. Conducted research and analyzed the properties of precast concrete. Summarized the history of precast concrete and the necessary components/processes for its successful development. The paper also addressed future potential applications currently being researched.

SUSTAINABILITY PROJECT. Performed a Life Cycle Analysis, by the U.S. Environmental Protection Agency standards, to exhibit the effectiveness of proposed sustainable alternative, Peracetic Acid and Ultraviolet Radiation Water Disinfection. This analysis included the four steps of LCA: goals and scope, inventory, impact assessment and interpretation. Calculations were tabulated to verify this effect.

SENIOR DESIGN PROJECT. Worked on a six-person group to design plans for the future Kalihi Middle Street Intermodal Transit Center. The site consisted of a transit center, handivan parking surface parking and a double helix parking structure. All plans were presented in a final submittal to the board, along with AutoCAD drawings.

PROFESSIONAL EXPERIENCE

ADMINISTRATIVE ASSISTANT INTERN	9/20xx – 7/20xx
Aflac Regional Office, Honolulu, HI	Salary: $10/hr
Supervisor: Dustin Deniz, 808-542-6884; may contact	20 hours/week

Provide customer service by responding to general customer inquiries and updating the status of claims. Created weekly reports for the Regional Coordinator from the four District Coordinators in regards to the present week's accomplishments and next week's goals.

POLITICAL CAMPAIGN VOLUNTEER   7/20xx-11/20xx
Carol Fukunaga Election Team, Honolulu, HI   Salary: $0.00
Supervisor: Renee Inouye, 808 783-3210; may contact   10 -15 hours/week

Raised awareness of policies or ideas that would improve the quality of life for people within the district. Worked and prepped campaign literature that was distributed at campaign office and in the Councilmember's district. Worked on improving campaign logistics to more effectively improve awareness of Councilwoman Fukunaga's community plans. Communicated with citizens to increase understanding of community problems that will be acted upon.

Key Accomplishments:
- Raised awareness for Councilmember's District 6 of new candidate running in a special election.
- Encouraged people in District 6 to vote in the special election.
- Councilwoman Fukunaga was in a field of 16 people. In the General Election in 20xx, she had more than 24.8 % of the votes, had 1,380+ votes over the second place runner, in a "winner take all' election.

OFFICE AUTOMATION CLERK   12/20xx – 6/20xx
U.S. Coast Guard 14th District, Honolulu, HI   Salary: $23,000
Supervisor: Debbie Vitale (retired), 808-842-2950   40 hours/week

Planned and sold transportation and accommodations to travel agency customers. Researched and booked reservations for travel destination activities. Marketed upcoming events and specials to customers.

TEACHER'S AIDE   9/20xx – 6/20xx
Mid-Pacific Institute Summer School, Honolulu, HI   Salary: $0.00
Supervisor: Marilyn Shigetani 808-973-5032; may contact   40 hours/week

Assisted to with tasks such as attendance, grading, preparing classroom materials and supervising elementary students.

LEADERSHIP AND VOLUNTEER EXPERIENCE

Holmes-coming UHM College of Engineering Networking Fundraiser   20xx-20xx
- As a member of the University of Hawaii at Manoa, American Society of Civil Engineers chapter, volunteered for UHM fundraiser. Staffed registration table and performed crowd control. Worked to meet attendees' expectations

UH Junior Engineering Expo   20xx, 20xx
- Emboldened middle school students to take an avid interest in the engineering profession with fun games and creative competition. Provided guidance and judged competitions.

Honolulu Marathon, Lead Assistant Volunteer   20xx-20xx
- Team leader
    o Checked in volunteers and showed volunteers where to go and what to do.
    o Prepped food and organized the activity.

Volunteer Construction Work   20xx-20xx
- Kalani High School: Participated in constructing and building cement benches. Benches were placed around the Kalani High School campus. Secured benches to the foundation.
- Mid-Pacific Institute: Participated in construction of sandbox for the elementary school. Helped lay the foundation, laid building cement tiles that built the sand box.

Veteran Applying for Special Agent Position After College

Dan joined the Marines right out of high school. He went to Afghanistan, was wounded in a firefight while posting security for a fellow Marine crossing a long open field, and was awarded a Purple Heart. He recovered from his injuries and decided that he was not going to just join the police department or stand at a security gate after separating from the military. Dan decided that he would get the qualifications required for Special Agent. He went to college on the GI Bill, got great grades, and is applying to Special Agent positions with federal agencies. The resume features security, team leadership, technical skills, critical thinking and experience that will match the qualifications for Special Agent. This resume was the first he had ever written.

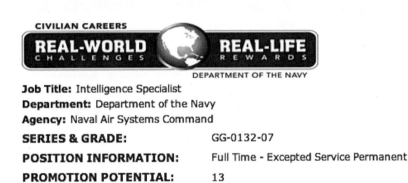

DEPARTMENT OF THE NAVY

Job Title: Intelligence Specialist
Department: Department of the Navy
Agency: Naval Air Systems Command

SERIES & GRADE:	GG-0132-07
POSITION INFORMATION:	Full Time - Excepted Service Permanent
PROMOTION POTENTIAL:	13

DUTIES:

- Employee performs **basic research and analysis** utilizing **all-source intelligence, databases, assessments, and/or products in support of assigned programs** within the Naval Aviation Enterprise (NAE), with a primary focus on intelligence support for Mission, Engineering, and Analysis; PEO Unmanned Aerial Vehicles and Cyber Threats.
- Participate in the **research, formulation, and presentation of oral briefings** and **written products for assigned customers** under the guidance of a senior analyst.
- The analyst will utilize **JWICS, to conduct research, communicate** with other analysts and subject matter experts, and utilize external **intelligence databases**.

QUALIFICATIONS REQUIRED:
In order to qualify for this position, your resume must provide sufficient experience and/or education, knowledge, skills, and abilities, to perform the duties of the specific position. Your resume is the key means we have for evaluating your skills, knowledge, and abilities, as they relate to this position. Therefore, we encourage you to be clear and specific when describing your experience.

Your resume must demonstrate at least one year of specialized experience at or equivalent to the GG/GS-07 grade level or pay band in the Federal service equivalent experience in the private or public sector. Specialized experience is defined as experience that is typically in or related to the work of the position to be filled and has equipped you with the particular knowledge, skills, and abilities to successfully perform the duties of the position. Specialized experience must demonstrate the following: **1) Research specific intelligence information in preparation of studies; 2) Extract all significant data pertaining to cyber-based intrusions; 3) Assist senior analysts with providing intelligence products.**

HOW YOU WILL BE EVALUATED:
When the application process is complete, we will review your resume to ensure you meet the hiring eligibility and qualification requirements listed in this announcement. You will be rated based on the information provided in your resume and responses to the questionnaire, along with your supporting documentation to determine your ability to demonstrate the following knowledge, skills and abilities/competencies:
- **RESEARCH**
- **INTELLIGENCE ANALYSIS**
- **INTELLIGENCE DATABASES**

DAN LOW
1108 Potomac Drive, Philadelphia, PA
Cell: (333) 333-3333 | Work: (333) 333-3333
Email: dkim101@gmail.com

Objective: Special Agent, Intelligence Analyst

EDUCATION

UNIVERSITY OF PENNSYLVANIA, Philadelphia, Pennsylvania (05/20xx)
Bachelor of Science Degree;   3.8 / 4.0 GPA
 COURSES: Comprehensive knowledge of Criminology, Constitutional and Criminal Law, Criminal Procedure and Rules of Evidence, Law Enforcement Philosophies and Techniques.

BALTIMORE COUNTY COMMUNITY COLLEGE, Baltimore, MD (06/20xx)
Associate of Science Degree; 3.7 / 4.0 GPA
 AWARDS: Phi Theta Kappa Honor Society Member, President's Honors

PROFESSIONAL EXPERIENCE:

RIFLEMAN (Rank: Lance Corporal)   **08/20xx – 07/ 20xx (one year)**
Marine Corps Base Hawaii, Kaneohe Bay, Hawaii
Supervisor: David Schaefer, 760-216-7239, may contact   40+ Hours per Week

 Participated in physical training and rifle range practices.

RIFLEMAN (Rank: Lance Corporal**)**   **02/20xx- 08/ 20xx (16 mos)**
Marine Corps, 2nd Battalion, Baghdad and Fallujah, Iraq
Supervisor: Capt Cedric Jefferson, 808-285-3507, may contact   40+ Hours per Week

 LEADERSHIP: Selected to supervise and motivate Marines in combat, ensuring mission success and troop welfare. Led a team of four soldiers on mounted security patrols. Organized and planned security around Iraqi checkpoints to search vehicles for weapons.

 COMMUNICATION/INTERPERSONAL ABILITY: Provided security for high-profile meetings at homes for the platoon commander and Iraqi sheikhs. Worked as part of a team that led a rigorous training program to teach Iraqi police personnel how to use U.S. weapons and tactics. Interacted with civilians, promoting cooperation and good will.

 SECURITY: Served as a primary scout, responsible for front line security. Provided foot and mobilized patrols of control points and the forward operating base. Provided the final barrier of an integrated security plan for asset(s) being protected. Also safely transported convicted Marines to the military jail or to the UCMJ military trial.

 FLEXIBILITY: Performed a variety of duties as assigned, to include conducting mounted security patrols, training Iraqi police personnel, serving as a primary scout, and transporting convicted Marines.

RIFLEMAN (Rank: Lance Corporal)   **09/2006-04/2007**
Marine Corps, 2nd Battalion, Al Haqlaniyah Haditha, Iraq
Supervisor: Capt, John Smith, 333-333-333, may contact   40+ Hours per Week

SECURITY: Served as a primary scout, responsible for front line security. Provided foot and mobilized patrols of control points, the K3 compound, and the forward operating base. Provided the final barrier of an integrated security plan for asset(s) being protected.

- Recognized for contributing to the success of 3rd platoon's mission by participating in numerous contacts, reconnaissance, ambushes, and security patrols conducted out of the Bani Dahir combat outpost and the forward operating base Haqlaniyah.
- Awarded the Purple Heart in 2007 for being wounded in a firefight while posting security for a Marine to cross a long open field.

COMBAT OPERATIONS: Deployed in support of the task force to the Haditha Triad, Iraq, for Operation Iraqi Freedom. Served as rifleman with assault troops and close combat forces. Conducted offensive tactics in confined spaces. Participated in dozens of combat patrols, made life and death decisions, continually improved my position, received enemy fire, and was subjected to the constant threat of improvised explosive devices (IEDs) and sniper rifles.

- As a member of the task force 2/3, answered the call to quell a fierce insurgency in the Haditha Triad. Deployed into the combat zone and participated in sustained operations against Ba'athists, Al Qaeda, and other associated terrorists.
- Awarded Combat Action Ribbon in recognition of having participated under enemy fire in ground combat firefight action.

SEARCH OPERATIONS: Conducted patrols and searches for high value target terrorists and IEDs in dangerous areas of the town. Conducted house searches based on intel and detailed known or suspected terrorists. Located high-powered sniper rifle and IED-making materials. Made identification cards for Iraqi civilians for the purpose of recording civilians living in towns and verifying they were not known or suspected terrorists.

- Recognized for being highly instrumental in targeted cordon and search operations in an attempt to capture suspected high value targets and weapons caches in the Al Anbar province in order to reduce the enemy footprint.

TRAINING AND CERTIFICATIONS

Military Academic Skills Program, 11/2008
Marine Rifleman: Combat Skills, 9/2007
Land Navigation, 9/2007
Infantry Patrolling, 7/2007
Fundamentals of Marine Corps Leadership, 6/2006
Infantry School, 3/2006
Combat Water Surface Survival, 08/2007
Advanced Aircraft Ditching, 8/2007

IPHABD Qualification, 8/2007
Basic Aircraft Ditching, 8/2007
Surface Survival, 8/2007
First Aid and CPR/AED; American Red Cross, 08/2014 (expires 08/2016)
Basic Martial Arts, Basic Military Science, Land Navigation/Tactical Operations, and Orienteering/Adventure Basic Training, 03/2005

AWARDS AND DECORATIONS

Purple Heart
Combat Action Ribbon
Navy Unit Commendation
Marine Corp Good Conduct Medal
National Defense Service Medal

Global War on Terrorism Service Medal
Iraq Campaign Medal
Sea Service Deployment Medal
Letter of Appreciation by Company Commander

LEVEL 4
make your resume straight fire

BE NITPICKY! Now it's time to pay attention to the little details that will make your resume look and read like a polished work.

check grammar and punctuation
proofread and edit
make your format consistent
spell check
... and then check some more!

TAKE ACTION!

Follow one of the samples from this book and create your resume. Be sure to proofread and have someone else proofread your resume. Your future employer, internship manager, or college admissions officer will not be impressed with any typos, grammatical errors, or inconsistencies in format.

RESUME TIPS

✔ State your objective carefully. An objective is optional but helpful. Your objective should state the type of position you desire.

✔ Keep the resume to one page if possible.

✔ Be sure your resume is error-free. Refer to the dictionary and your grammar books as needed. Run your software's spell checker.

✔ Beware of spell checkers. They won't catch errors in which you have used the wrong word, such as "there" instead of "their."

✔ To check each word's spelling, start at the bottom and read your sentences backwards. You will pick up words that don't make sense. This helps you focus on each word and not be distracted by the context.

✔ Have a friend, teacher, or parent read your resume to make sure the grammar, the punctuation, and all details are correct and consistent. This is extremely important! You can easily miss errors in simple things such as your phone number and employment dates.

✔ Use good white or off-white cotton bond paper.

✔ If you mail your resume, include your return address on the cover letter and on the top-left corner of the envelope.

✔ On the envelope, write a brief description of what is enclosed. For example, you might write "Enclosed: Application for Cashier Position."

✔ Always be honest.

✘ Don't include your birth date or a photograph of yourself. Equal Employment Opportunity laws state that employers cannot discriminate against people because of their demographics. Including information about your age or a picture that shows your race places the employer in an awkward position.

✘ Don't include statements about your health, unless you're applying for a physical job.

✘ Don't include your Social Security number. Give it to an employer on your application if requested. If you apply for a federal government internship, you will have to add your Social Security number on the application.

✘ Avoid writing anything negative. You don't have to tell the employer everything, so don't include less-than flattering information, such as negative reasons for leaving a job or a low grade-point average.

Online Builders and Templates

Get ready to copy and paste your resume into online applications, resume builders and templates. It's best if you first write the resume in a word processing application, such as Microsoft Word, so that you won't have the "time-out" problem or lose your content.

✔ Use 12-point type.

✔ Use ALL CAPS (just 2-4 words) headings for emphasizing headings, job titles, or other important information.

✔ Include keywords and skills that are of interest to the employer.

✔ After you copy and paste your paragraph into an online form, review for line breaks. Fix lines that are broken incorrectly.

✔ Be consistent in the number of returns between headings.

✔ Be consistent in using ALL CAPS headings and titles.

✔ Proofread carefully.

✔ Preview your resume to fix any formatting problems.

✘ Don't use bold type.

✘ Don't indent or center any type.

✘ Don't use the automatic bullet feature in Word.

Paper Resumes

A paper format resume is best for mailing or handing to a manager. You can also attach your paper format resume to an e-mail as a Microsoft Word file. You can usually upload Word documents to online resume databases, too. The paper format resume is better looking, easier to read, and more impressive than the electronic resume.

The average length of time a person will spend reviewing your resume is 3 to 10 seconds. People are busy and have short attention spans. You will hold their attentions only if your resume is attractive, well-organized, and error-free. If your resume is disorganized or has any mistakes, the employer will probably just throw it away.

You can find free and inexpensive templates online or search for resume designs online for inspiration. This book features several template designs from **Hloom.com**, which has nearly 300 free templates to download into Word.

A good layout can enhance the content of your resume. An employer's eye will go to the top and center of the page, so your contact information should be in that position. Put other important details (such as your skills section) near the top of your resume to ensure that they will be read. Information at the bottom might be overlooked.

Type Style

Bold, *italic*, ***bold italic***, ALL CAPS, and SMALL CAPS are type styles that you can use to emphasize certain text on your resume. Be consistent. For example, if you use bold and all caps for one job title, use bold and all caps for every job title.

Point Size

Point size refers to the size of the letters. Typically, 12-point type is used for resumes; 11-point type is acceptable if needed. You can set your name in larger type so that it stands out. The headings for your resume could be in 12-point type with the rest of the resume in 11-point type for extra emphasis on the headings.

Margins

The usual margins are 1 to 1.25 inches at the top and bottom and on both sides. You can adjust these according to how much text you have.

Paragraphs

Paragraphs can be written in block style or with bullets to highlight every sentence, as you see in the following examples.

Layout

Layout is the overall design of the resume. It includes the placement and alignment of various elements of your resume. Be consistent with your layout. For example, use the same amount of spacing between each section of your resume.

White Space

White space between and around sections of your resume makes your resume easier to read. Between resume sections, allow a return. Spacing between employer names and job titles can also be a return if space permits. Too much white space causes a resume to look skimpy. Too little space makes it look busy and cluttered.

Format Your Resume for Easy Reading

ACTIVITIES ASSISTANT, Goddard School, Chesterfield, VA, August 20xx to present; 20 hours per week
- SCHEDULING: Create and organize a planned schedule for the week to come. Coordinate with other teachers and specialists to organize student schedule for daily activities.
- CHILDCARE SUPERVISION: Supervise a full classroom of 18 kindergarteners. Interact and communicate with parents on a daily basis.

ADMINISTRATIVE ASSISTANT, GSI Commerce, Melbourne, FL, December 20xx to June 20xx
- DATA ENTRY: Performed data input and analysis for catalog marketing company.
- CUSTOMER SERVICE: Provided top-notch customer service; effectively responded to customer concerns and questions.

MAUI RETAIL CORP., Lahaina, Maui, 20xx–present
RETAIL SALES / COMPUTER ASSISTANT to the Regional Manager

COMPUTER RESEARCH: Research inventory, costs, and store information. Research competitive companies, products, and catalogs via the Internet. SALES REPORTS: Manipulate online data to create sales and financial reports. Develop formulas and create Excel spreadsheets, graphs, and reports for management and financial analysis by managers. SALES AND CUSTOMER SERVICE: Conducted retail sales, friendly customer service, inventory control, and merchandising.

write a legit cover letter

IN YOUR COVER LETTER, SUMMARIZE THE BEST OF WHAT YOU HAVE TO OFFER.

Today, cover letters can be on paper or delivered as email. The content is about the same either way. Today's hiring and human resources managers are very busy. You have only a few seconds to impress them. Your cover letter is another opportunity to pitch your interest, skills, and qualifications for the position.

Why write a cover letter?

- Get the reader's attention.
- Impress the employer.
- Use keywords and skills from the job announcement.
- Show your genuine interest in the company and its customers.
- Show that you are enthusiastic, energetic, dependable, professional, and determined.

Your cover letter should include:

1. Your contact information
2. The employer's contact information
3. Greeting
4. Intro paragraph
5. Middle paragraph with important skills
6. Closing paragraph with logistics information
7. Signature and attachments

Use the cover letter to highlight experiences that are of interest to the employer. You can highlight an important accomplishment, such as being a champion swimmer, playing a main role in the school play, or pitching for the school's baseball team. Potential employers will see you as a person with energy and enthusiasm. Hopefully, they will want to meet you and see whether you have the same enthusiasm in person.

Cover Letter Sample

KALIN C. SMYTHE
4404 Allison Drive / Baltimore, MD 21229
(410) 999-9999 / kalinsmythe@net.com

Subject: KALIN C. SMYTHE, Interested in Barista Position

Dear Ms. Singerman,

I was referred to you by my friend Jason Sparks, who works in your downtown location. He speaks very highly of the employee-friendly work environment there and thinks I would be a good addition to the team.

I am a junior in high school and have retail experience. I would like to be a member of a barista team in the Seattle area. My important skills for this position include the following:

- I love coffee and have a good memory for complex orders.
- I am also fast-moving and efficient and can keep up with peak customer service times.

I am available to work 20 hours per week, including weekends during the summer. I can also work flexible hours. I have a car, so my transportation is covered. Thank you for your consideration. I hope to hear from you soon.

Sincerely,
KALIN C. SMYTHE

Enclosure: resume

See more cover letter samples on pages 37 and 45.

 **USE OUR FREE COVER LETTER BUILDER!**
www.resume-place.com/cover-letter-builder/

LEVEL 6

apply for jobs like a pro

FOLLOW DIRECTIONS CAREFULLY!

In some cases, you are not finished with the entire application by submitting just a resume. With employment and internship opportunities, as well as college applications, you will probably have to complete an application (often online), answer essay questions, and write a personal statement. You also need to send a cover letter. College, job, internship, co-op, work-study, and workshop opportunities are very competitive, and recruiters and admissions committees ask for more information from you than just a resume in many cases. You will have to follow the directions, take the time to complete the full application, write your narratives, and submit it all correctly.

Application Forms

Many internship, job, and work-study applications are posted online. The online applications, profile set-up, resume submissions, and pre-screening questionnaires are complex. If you cannot fill out an application online correctly, you may not get an interview or hired. Take your time and follow all the directions.

PreScreening Questions

*1.Are you currently authorized to work for all US employers in any position on a full time basis, or are you only authorized for your current employer?

    Authorized for all US employers   ▼

*2.What country are you applying to work in?

    US   ▼

*3.To better direct your resume, select the area within Target that interests you.

    Target Stores   ▼

*4.If you are able to relocate, what area(s) within the US are you interested in?

    I am not able to relocate ▲
    East

Be patient. Sometimes you can upload your resume, but employers usually prefer the resume builders.

Most important piece of advice: Follow the directions carefully. This is a test!

When filling out applications:

- Take your time. Copy and paste when you can from your Word resume.

- Use only the space allowed for descriptions of work experiences. If the space is small, keep your descriptions short. If you need to include longer descriptions, attach your resume.

- Fill in all the blanks. If they ask for supervisors or references, be sure to add them. Keep a list of references, phone numbers, and email addresses available for applications.

- Include your educational activities and honors. Usually you can add these into an "other information" field toward the end of the application.

- Write a short statement in the "other information" field about why you would like to have this position and the skills you can bring to the job, or attach a cover letter.

- Proofread to make sure there are no typos.

- Be consistent with writing style, capitalization, and grammar.

Work Experience

List the work experiences below, starting with the most recent one.

Work Experience 1
☑ Current Job

Employer
The Resume Place, Inc.
Select

Job Title
Customer Services

Start Date
Mar ▾ | 2013 ▾

Tasks & Achievements
Communications with Customers

Reason for Leaving
Increased salary

Questionnaires & Essays

The questions in the following sample application are basically interview questions. The employer is giving you a chance to think about working for them and what would be most important in doing that. Your answers to these questions, plus your resume, decide whether you'll get an actual interview for a position. Questions and narrative answers are becoming an important part of the job application process today. Hiring managers and recruiters can read your answers and decide whether they like your writing and critical-thinking skills.

- Be sure to answer the question.

- Study the company's mission or the college philosophy to make sure you have a similar mission or philosophy.

- Add enthusiasm, energy, congeniality, and motivation to your answers. A positive attitude is impressive, winning, engaging, and attention getting.

- Pick out the important keywords from the question. Use those keywords in your answer, to make sure you have answered it correctly in the language of the company or college.

- Give examples of your own academic or other experience that demonstrate your interest in the job.

- Use the personal pronoun "I" with your answer because these are personal narrative statements.

- Proofread, edit, and make sure the answers are written well. This is actually a writing and critical-thinking test.

- Have someone else read the questions and answers to make sure the answers are well written and not too long.

College, Scholarship, or Internship Essays

Your college application essay is an important narrative about your interest in the school and your background. College recruiters look for well-written narratives about candidates' experiences that will contribute to the success of those candidates at their colleges.

When writing college entrance essays, do the following:

- Give dates and a reference for your examples (in case the reader doesn't have your resume).

- Tell a story or give an anecdote about yourself.

- Write about the lessons you have learned.

- Write about something you are proud of in your high school career.

- Write about challenges that you overcame and how you overcame them.

- Write about your vision for yourself as a college student and your future career.

- Have someone edit and proofread your narrative.

- Write in first person—use the personal pronoun "I."

- Follow the narrative length and application instructions carefully.

- This is a writing test, so consider this as a significant research paper.

The following is an example of an essay topic and an appropriate response. Review it to see what this applicant did right. Also, consider responding to the topic yourself with your own essay for practice.

WRITE YOUR STORIES AND INTERESTS

Topic: How I have grown and changed since my freshman year of high school and the experiences that have fostered my development as a person.

My first year at Mount St. Joseph High School was a difficult one for me. All of my close friends had chosen to attend another high school. As a freshman, I found myself following the crowd and making choices that others would accept, not necessarily the choices I would have preferred. I tried out for the basketball team and at first was not chosen.

But in the Spring of my freshman year, I was successful in making the JV Golf Team, which proved to be a turning point for me. The person I am today is a result of personal success and growth, as well as my failures. My participation on the golf team helped me to develop patience and persistence, and to be positive, win or lose.

This year, I was one of 20 students chosen to participate in a weeklong service project in a very poor community in rural Virginia. Our job for the week was to repair homes and clean up the community. The residents' homes were in terrible shape and did not even have indoor plumbing. I was in utter shock to learn that in an area so close to my home, there are people who cannot afford indoor plumbing.

The week I spent in Cape Charles proved to be one of the most significant experiences of my life. It helped me realize how much I take for granted in my life and how important it is to help others. The people were so appreciative of our help. Even though they were very poor, they were also very generous, and they offered to share what little they did have with our group. This amazing experience not only affected my personal outlook on life but reinforced my commitment to community service.

As a freshman, I hesitated to be a leader and to make my own decisions for fear of what my peers might say. As a senior preparing to meet a whole new set of risks and challenges, I feel I have learned a lot from my high school experiences. My participation in school sports, clubs, leadership programs, and community service has influenced how I see the world and how I interact with others. It has also helped me to become a better person. Today, I am more self-confident and not afraid to take risks. I consider myself a leader rather than a follower and I am more committed to helping others.

interview on point

BE PREPARED!

Once you've gotten through the first round of applying, some employers or colleges will request an interview. The interview is your chance to show the employer/recruiter what you're all about. There are several different formats for interviews, but with these easy tips, you'll nail it!

INTERVIEW TIPS

before the interview

- Be prepared!
- Check out the website of the organization you're interviewing with and conduct research (size, services, products, etc.).

PREPARE A ONE-MINUTE RESPONSE TO THE "TELL ME ABOUT YOURSELF" QUESTION

- Be memorable! Media training expert TJ Walker from www.worldwidemedia.com recommends that you have a story or message prepared so that you will be remembered at the "water cooler".
- Write five success stories to answer behavioral interview questions ("Tell me about a time when…" or "Give me an example of a time…").
- Prepare answers to the most common interview questions that will best present your skills, talents, and accomplishments:
    - Why did you leave your last position?
    - What do you know about our organization?
    - What are your goals/Where do you see yourself in 5 years?
    - What are your strengths? What are your weaknesses/areas of improvement?
    - Why would you like to work for this organization?
    - What is your most significant achievement?
    - How would your last boss/colleagues/friends describe you?
    - Why should we hire you?
    - What are your salary expectations?
- Remember, nothing will make you look worse than not knowing what you put on your own resume.
- Have 5-10 high quality questions prepared for the interviewer. Only ask the ones that were not addressed during your discussion.
- Practice in front of a mirror or with a friend for feedback.
- Have your references' permission. These might be former managers, professors, or people who know you through community service. You want them to be prepared to praise you. It would be beneficial to provide your references with the following information: the job for which you are applying, the name of the organization, and a copy of your resume.

during the in-person interview

- Wear an outfit that fits the company's image (no jeans). You should be dressed similarly to the way everyone else at the company dresses. If you are in doubt about how the people at the company will be dressed, dress as nicely as possible.

- Be confident. Remember that the company wants to hire a good employee or intern.

- Think positively.

- Show up a few minutes early. Don't get stressed out trying to find the location. Sound upbeat and hopeful for a position. It's okay to say you're good at a few things.

- Let the interviewer know why the company should hire you. Look at your resume just before you go in the door so that you will remember your skills and experience.

- Express that you would like to get experience doing this work.

- Look the interviewer in the eye. Don't look down too often.

GIVE GOOD EYE CONTACT

SMILE!

BE CONFIDENT

THINK POSITIVELY

DON'T PUT YOUR HANDS IN YOUR POCKETS

- Sit in a similar fashion to the interviewer. It's better to lean forward toward the interviewer.

- Breathe naturally and relax.

- Keep your resume in an attractive folder, not crumpled in your pocket or purse.

- Do not take a backpack, athletic bag, water bottle, book, or huge purse to an interview. Take only a small folder or notebook.

- Update your resume before the interview so that the interviewer does not have to ask questions that waste time.

- Bring a pen and notepad. Take a few notes during the interview. You will need these notes for writing your thank-you letter. Be sure to get the correct spelling and pronunciation of the interviewer's name and his or her title. Get a business card if you can.

Be ready to answer questions. Also, prepare a few questions of your own while you are studying the organization's website. Try to ask two or three questions (other than "What does the job pay?").

- Watch your posture and don't put your hands in your pockets.

- Do not speak negatively of yourself or a former employer. Skip all the bad history.

- Do not bring food, drink, or gum to an interview.

- Be polite. Say thank you after the interview and smile.

- It's okay to ask when the hiring manager will be making a decision about the position.

- Don't ask about salary or benefits at the first interview. Wait to see whether the interviewer is going to call you back or offer you a position. Ask about salary and benefits at that time, before you accept the position.

TURN OFF YOUR CELL PHONE AND OTHER ELECTRONIC DEVICES, OR DON'T BRING THEM AT ALL.

8

follow up: keep it 100

FINISH STRONG!

Don't just send in your resume and forget about it, or leave an interview without another word. You can still take a few actions to demonstrate that you are genuinely interested in the position, to show that you have excellent interpersonal skills, and to learn more about how your resume and application measured up.

TAKE ACTION!

After you submit your resume, follow up in a week or two with an email or phone call.

After you have an interview, send a thank-you note to the interviewer.

After you submit a resume for a federal job, check USAJOBS.gov for the status of your application and find out why it was rejected if it was.

get organized

Follow-up requires setting up a way to track the applications you have submitted, the responses to your application, and the follow-up actions you have taken or should take. Create a file on your computer to keep this information organized.

You can also use this file or a separate file to manage your job hunting network, the people you know who you could contact for job leads and information. Keep track of names, email addresses, phone numbers, job titles, companies, and how you know each person. The information they provide could result in jobs, interviews, mentoring opportunities, and establishing excellent references.

give them a call

You can call the contact person listed on the job announcement. Practice you will say before you call, and also practice what you will say if they available and you need to leave a voicemail message.

Sample Voicemail Message Script

"Hello, I'm Nicole Smith, I'm calling regarding my application for Retail Sales. I'm checking on the interview results. I can be reached at 410 744 4324 from 9am until 9 pm, or you can text me. Thanks so much for your consideration. I would really like to work for Target."

say thanks!

You won't include a thank-you letter with your resume, obviously, but these documents are still integral to the application process. Do you want to be remembered after an interview? Sending a thank-you letter is the best way to accomplish this. The thank-you letter is a great opportunity to get your name in front of the interviewer again. You will have the chance to tell the person how much you appreciate his or her time and how much you like the organization. You can also reiterate that you would like to work for the interviewer's company.

Email thank-you notes are very effective!

A few tips:

- Make your letter genuine.

- Employers like to know that you noticed their businesses, employees, and customers. When you're in an interview, pay attention to your surroundings. Find something you like and mention it in your thank-you letter.

- Always put your name in the subject line. For example:
  Thank You from [Your Name]

EXAMPLES

Dear Ms. Singerman,
Thank you for your introduction to the Cool Beans team yesterday. I believe I would fit in with the team as an excellent barista because of my ability to multitask, because I am friendly with customers, and because I have a good memory for orders. I am available to begin work next Monday.
Thanks again!
Sincerely,
KALIN C. SMYTHE

Dear Mr. Suites,

Thank you very much for your time on Monday. I am very interested in your hotel management training program. I am available to begin work in two weeks. I look forward to hearing from you soon.

Sincerely,
Emily Nopolus

got an offer! wow! awesome! now what?

GREAT! You did it! If you receive an offer, know that you can sometimes negotiate a job or internship offer. Here are some tips to keep in mind, before you accept.

- Thank the person enthusiastically for the offer.

- Listen to the offer carefully. Take notes if you can.

- Ask any questions that you may have about hours, responsibilities, salary, training, benefits, and challenges.

- Tell this person you would like one day to think about the position. If possible, it's always best not to accept the offer immediately. Make sure the job is right for you before you accept. Ask more questions if needed.

- You might be able to negotiate the salary or other benefits if your qualifications are excellent.

- You can also ask for additional training, courses, travel, or opportunities within the position.

- If you are asking for a different hourly rate or salary or additional benefits, you will need to be prepared to negotiate. Making a list of why you believe you should earn a few more dollars could be successful. You might want to present your best qualifications again. You can cite your education, experience, and skills.

- Call back the next day. Say you are very pleased by the offer and either accept the offer, reject the offer, or present your requests.

What Will Happen Now?

The hiring manager will consider your ideas. They will consider their offer and your requests and may come back with a different offer (or not). Then, you get to decide whether you will take the position. If you do: congratulations, you are hired!

INDEX

W

White space, 55
Work Experience section, 7
Work experiences, 59
Writing jobs, 22, 23, 30

Z

Zoo visitor center positions, 14

TEN STEPS TO A FEDERAL JOB® CERTIFICATION PROGRAM

Since 1992, over 2,000 career professionals have benefited from our unique certification in the Ten Steps to a Federal Job® curriculum, and the program continues to grow each year. Get certified and licensed to teach Kathryn Troutman's popular, proven, turnkey curriculum: Ten Steps to a Federal Job® and Federal Resume & KSA Writing curriculum. This course was developed by Kathryn Troutman as a direct result of her training experiences at hundreds of federal agencies throughout the world.

Our three-day program is pre-approved to fulfill 24 continuing education hours for the Center of Credentialing and Education's Global Career Development Facilitator (GCDF) certification.

Registration Benefits - Incredible Value!

- Federal Career Books for Your Library:
  ◊ *Federal Resume Guidebook*
  ◊ *Jobseeker's Guide*
  ◊ *The New SES Application*
  ◊ *Creating Your First Resume*
  ◊ Beautiful Ten Steps bag

- PowerPoint Presentations for your use as a trainer:
  ◊ Ten Steps to a Federal Job® – Licensed for three years
  ◊ Federal Hiring Program
  ◊ Veteran's and Spouse Hiring Programs
  ◊ Student Federal Hiring Programs

"I just wanted to let you know that attendance at the three-day course has done wonders for my confidence and wonders for my clients. When we go through the OPM Job Factors and the Grading of GS positions, most clients are over-joyed to have opened the "treasure chest" where the mystery of pursuing a Federal Job Position is solved. Thank you for all that you do!! I love the books and find something new EVERY day that I can share with my fellow coaches."

CERTIFIED
Federal Job
Search Trainer™

CERTIFIED
Federal Career
Coach™

More Information and Registration
www.fedjobtraining.com/certification-programs.htm

Award-Winning, Best-Selling Career Books by Kathryn Troutman

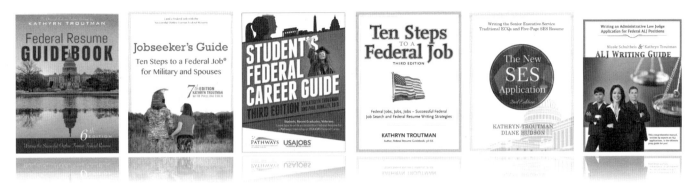

FEDERAL RESUME GUIDEBOOK 6th Edition—Perfect for federal-to-federal jobseekers. This book has comprehensive, in-depth guidance on how to craft the perfect federal application to change jobs or get promoted. The *Federal Resume Guidebook* is THE book that created today's federal resume.

JOBSEEKER'S GUIDE 7th Edition—The *Jobseeker's Guide* is the first-ever publication for military and family members who are seeking federal employment. This best-selling publication is the accepted training handout in Transition GPS classes and employment courses at Military Transition Centers worldwide and is utilized in more than 100 military bases around the world. This publication is also the featured guide supporting the Certified Federal Job Search Trainer program for career counselors on the Ten Steps to a Federal Job®.

THE NEW SES APPLICATION 2nd Edition—The SES job application is complex. *The New SES Application* breaks it down into a step-by-step process based on a popular workshop taught for over 10 years. Tackle the traditional ECQs and the SES Federal Resume with confidence.

TEN STEPS TO A FEDERAL JOB 3rd Edition—Wouldn't it be great to have all the basic steps you need to land that dream federal job in just one book? *Ten Steps to a Federal Job* is that book, and with the 3rd edition, Kathryn Troutman outdid herself by adding new crucial details and background on the federal job search that you won't find anywhere else! Learn the tips and tricks to convert your private-industry resume into a winning federal format.

STUDENT'S FEDERAL CAREER GUIDE 3rd Edition—This book is a must-buy for students, new graduates, young professionals, parents, college career centers, and career counselors. Details the winning 10-step process for going from the classroom to a federal job. Includes basics like our federal employment glossary, tips on salary negotiation, and a step-by-step guide to the behavior-based interview.

Published by the Federal Career Training Institute
A Division of The Resume Place, Inc.

More information and secure online ordering:
www.fedjobtraining.com
(888) 480-8265 ext. 2 Mon - Fri 9am - 5pm ET
Get the Publisher's Best Price for Bulk Orders